D1590848

Ah, This!

Published by
Rajneesh Foundation International
Rajneeshpuram, Oregon 97741 U.S.A.

Bhagwan
Shree
Rajneesh

Ah,
This!

Responses to disciples'
and visitors' questions
and Zen stories

Published by Ma Anand Sheela
Rajneesh Foundation International
Rajneeshpuram
Oregon 97741
USA

First Edition December 1982
7,000 copies

Printed in USA

ISBN 0-88050-502-8
Library of Congress Catalog Card Number 82-24026

Contents

Introduction

A raincloud shrouds the valley.
Night rains have filled the air with sage.
Past my window, a tumbleweed spins
and, in the stream, a gray heron stands, poised to
strike.
The morning sun rolls over dark hills.

On and on, wherever I look, beauty, wonder.
I could say, "This is God,"
or try to tell you about Zen
or the Zen Master whose book this is.
My head could talk to your head.
But why?
The Master has said it all
better than I,
and now lives in silence,
occasionally murmuring,
"Ah, this!"

To all our questions:
What is enlightenment?
Who am I?
What is the meaning of life?
Does God exist?
What is reality?
He waves his hand and says, "This!"
What is "this?" YOU are. Look, smell, taste, listen, touch—all at once. Feel, laugh, jump, run, shout, breathe. Breathe it in, breathe it out. It's all you. This, black letters on white paper changing into a word with a meaning in your brain, is you now. You, trying to grasp it, is this. Whatever is, right now, right here, for you is this. This is all there is.
Hence Zen Master Daie says, "All the teachings the sages expounded are no more than commentaries on your sudden cry: "Ah, this!"

Swami Prem Pramod

The discourses in this book,
based on Zen stories
and questions and answers
were given by Bhagwan Shree Rajneesh
at the Shree Rajneesh Ashram, Poona, India
January 3 - 10, 1980

Ascending to the high seat, Dogen Zenji said:
"Zen Master Hogen studied with Keishin Zenji.

Once Keishin Zenji asked him,
'Joza, where do you go?'

Hogen said, 'I am making pilgrimage aimlessly.'

Keishin said, 'What is the matter of your pilgrimage?'

Hogen said, 'I don't know.'

Keishin said, 'Not knowing is the most intimate.'

Hogen suddenly attained great enlightenment."

The Heart
of Knowing
is Now

*Z*EN IS JUST ZEN. There is nothing comparable to it. It is unique—unique in the sense that it is the most ordinary and yet the most extraordinary phenomenon that has happened to human consciousness. It is the most ordinary because it does not believe in knowledge, it does not believe in mind. It is not a philosophy, not a religion either. It is the acceptance of the ordinary existence with a total heart, with one's total being, not desiring some other world, supra-mundane, supra-mental. It has no interest in any esoteric nonsense, no interest in metaphysics at all. It does not hanker for the other shore; this shore is more than enough. Its acceptance of this shore is so tremendous that through that very acceptance it transforms this shore—and *this* very shore becomes the other shore:

> *This very body the Buddha;*
> *This very earth the Lotus Paradise.*

Hence it is ordinary. It does not want you to create a certain kind of spirituality, a certain kind of holiness. All that it asks is that you live your life with immediacy, spontaneity. And then the mundane becomes the sacred.

The great miracle of Zen is in the transformation of the mundane into the sacred. And it is tremendously extraordinary because *this* way life has never been approached before, *this* way life has never been respected before.

Zen goes beyond Buddha and beyond Lao Tzu. It is a culmination, a transcendence, both of the Indian genius and of the Chinese genius. The Indian genius reached its highest peak in Gautam the Buddha and the Chinese genius reached its highest peak in Lao Tzu. And the meeting . . . the essence of Buddha's teaching and the essence of Lao Tzu's teaching merged into one stream so deeply that no separation is possible now. Even to make a distinction between what belongs to Buddha and what to Lao Tzu is impossible, the merger has been so total. It is not only a synthesis, it is an integration. Out of this meeting Zen was born. Zen is neither Buddhist nor Taoist and yet both.

To call Zen "Zen Buddhism" is not right because it is far more. Buddha is not so earthly as Zen is. Lao Tzu is tremendously earthly, but Zen is not only earthly: its vision transforms the earth into heaven. Lao Tzu is earthly, Buddha is unearthly, Zen is both—and in being both it has become the most extraordinary phenomenon.

The future of humanity will go closer and closer to the approach of Zen, because the meeting of the East and West is possible only through something like Zen, which is earthly and yet unearthly. The West is very earthly, the East is very unearthly. Who is going to become the bridge? Buddha cannot be the bridge; he is so essentially Eastern, the very flavor of the East, the very fragrance of the East, uncompromising. Lao Tzu cannot be the bridge; he is too earthly. China has always been very earthly. China is more part of the Western psyche than of the Eastern psyche.

It is not an accident that China is the first country in the East to turn communist, to become materialist, to believe in a godless philosophy, to believe that man is only matter and nothing else. This is not just accidental. China has been earthly for almost five thousand years; it is very Western. Hence Lao Tzu cannot become the bridge; he is more like Zorba the Greek. Buddha is so unearthly you cannot even catch hold of him—how can he become the bridge?

When I look all around, Zen seems to be the only possibility, because in Zen, Buddha and Lao Tzu have become one. The meeting has already happened. The seed is there, the seed of that great bridge which can make East and West one. Zen is going to be the meeting-point. It has a great future—a great past and a great future.

And the miracle is that Zen is neither interested in the past nor in the future. Its total interest is in the present. Maybe that's why the miracle is possible, because the past and the future are bridged by the present.

The present is not part of time. Have you ever thought about it? How long is the present? The past has a duration, the future has a duration. What is the duration of the present? How long does it last? Between the past and the future can you measure the present? It is immeasurable; it is almost not. It is not time at all: it is the penetration of eternity into time.

And Zen lives in the present. The whole teaching is: how to be in the present, how to get out of the past which is no more and how not to get involved in the future which is not yet, and just to be rooted, centered, in that which is.

The whole approach of Zen is of immediacy, but because of that it can bridge the past and the future. It can bridge many things: it can bridge the past and the future, it can bridge the East and the West, it can bridge body and soul. It can bridge the unbridgeable worlds: this world and that, the mundane and the sacred.

BEFORE WE ENTER INTO this small anecdote it will be good to understand a few things. The first: the Masters do not tell the truth. Even if they want to they cannot; it is impossible. Then what is their function? What do they go on doing? They cannot tell the truth, but they can call forth the truth which is fast asleep in you. They can provoke it, they can challenge it. They can shake you up, they can wake you up. They cannot *give* you God, truth, *nirvana,* because in the first place you already have it all with you. You are born with it. It is innate, it is intrinsic. It is your very nature.   So anybody who pretends to give you the truth is simply exploiting your stupidity, your gullibility. He is cunning—cunning and utterly ignorant too. He knows nothing; not even a glimpse of truth has happened to him. He is a pseudo Master.

Truth cannot be given; it is already in you. It can be called forth, it can be provoked. A context can be created, a certain space can be created in which it rises in you and is no more asleep, becomes awakened.

The function of the Master is far more complex than you think. It would have been far easier, simpler, if truth could be conveyed. It cannot be conveyed, hence indirect ways and means have to be devised.

The New Testament has the beautiful story of Lazarus. Christians have missed the whole point of it. Christ is so unfortunate—he has fallen into the wrong company. Not even a single Christian theologian has been able to discover the meaning of the story of Lazarus, his death and resurrection.

Lazarus dies. He is the brother of Mary Magdalene and Martha and a great devotee of Jesus. Jesus is far away; by the time he gets the information and the invitation, "Come immediately," two days have already passed, and by the time he reaches Lazarus' place four days have passed. But Mary and Martha are waiting for him—their trust is such. The whole village is laughing at them. They are being stupid in others' eyes because they are keeping the corpse in a cave; they are watching day in, day out, guarding the corpse. The corpse has already started stinking; it is deteriorating.

The village people are saying, "You are fools! Jesus cannot do anything. When somebody is dead, somebody is dead!"

Jesus comes. He goes to the cave—he does not enter into the cave—he stands outside and calls Lazarus forth. The people have gathered. They must be laughing: "This man seems to be crazy!"

Somebody says to him, "What are you doing?" He is dead! He has been dead for four days. In fact, to enter into the cave is difficult—his body is stinking. It is impossible! Whom are you calling?"

But, unperturbed, Jesus shouts again and again, "Lazarus, come out!"

And the crowd is in for a great surprise: Lazarus

walks out of the cave—shaken, shocked, as if out of a great slumber, as if he had fallen into a coma. He himself cannot believe what has happened, why he is in the cave.

This in fact is just a way of saying what the function of a Master is. Whether Lazarus was really dead or not is not the point. Whether Jesus was capable of raising the dead or not is not the point. To get involved in those stupid questions is absurd. Only scholars can be so foolish. No man of understanding will think that this is something historical. It is far more! It is not a fact, it is a truth. It is not something that happens in time, it is something more: something that happens in eternity.

You are all dead. You are all in the same situation as Lazarus. You are all living in your dark caves. You are all stinking and deteriorating. . . because death is not something that comes one day suddenly—you are dying every day. Since the day of your birth you have been dying. It is a long process; it takes seventy, eighty, ninety years to complete it. *Each moment* something of you dies, something in you dies, but you are absolutely unaware of the whole situation. You go on as if you are alive; you go on living as if you know what life is.

The function of the Master is to call forth: "Lazarus, come out of the cave! Come out of your grave! Come out of your death!"

The Master cannot give you the truth but he can call forth the truth. He can stir something in you. He can trigger a process in you which will ignite a fire, a flame. Truth you are—just so much dust has gathered around you. The function of the Master is negative: he has to give you a bath, a shower, so the dust disappears.

That's exactly the meaning of Christian baptism.

That's what John the Baptist was doing in the River Jordan. But people go on misunderstanding. Today also baptism happens in the churches; it is meaningless.

John the Baptist was preparing people for an inner bath. When they were ready he would take them symbolically into the River Jordan. That was only symbolic—just as your orange clothes are symbolic, that bath in the River Jordan was symbolic—symbolic that the Master can give you a bath. He can take the dust, the dust of centuries, away from you. And suddenly all is clear, all is clarity. That clarity is enlightenment.

The great Master Daie says: *"All the teachings of the sages, of the saints, of the Masters, have expounded no more than this: they are commentaries on your sudden cry, 'Ah, this!' "*

When suddenly you are clear and a great joy and rejoicing arises in you, and your whole being, every fiber of your body, mind and soul dances, and you say, "Ah, this! Alleluia!" a great shout of joy arises in your being, that is enlightenment. Suddenly stars come down from the rafters. You become part of the eternal dance of existence.

Auden says:

Dance till the stars come down from the rafters!
Dance, dance, dance till you drop!

Yes, it happens—it is not something that you have to do. It is something that even if you want not to do you will find it impossible; you will find it impossible to resist. You will have to dance.

The beauty of this, the beauty of now, the joy that existence is and the closeness of it. . . . Yes, stars come down from the rafters. They are so close you can just touch them; you can hold them in your hands.

Daie is right. He says:

All the teachings the sages expounded are no more than commentaries on your sudden cry, "Ah, this!"

The whole heart saying "Aha!" And the silence that follows it, and the peace, and the joy, and the meeting, and the merger, and the orgasmic experience, the ecstasy . . . !

Masters don't teach the truth; there is no way to teach it. It is a transmission beyond scriptures, beyond words. It is a transmission. It is energy provoking energy in you. It is a kind of synchronicity.

The Master has disappeared as an ego; he is pure joy. And the disciple sits by the side of the Master slowly slowly partaking of his joy, of his being, eating and drinking out of that eternal, inexhaustible source: *ais dhammo sanantano.* And one day . . . and one cannot predict when that day will come; it is unpredictable. One day suddenly it has happened: a process has started in you which reveals the truth of your being to you. You come face to face with yourself. God is not somewhere else: he is now, here.

The Masters illuminate and confirm realization. They illuminate in a thousand and one ways. They go on pointing towards the truth: fingers pointing to the moon. But there are many fools who start clinging to the fingers. By clinging to the fingers you will not see the moon, remember. There are even greater fools who start biting the fingers. That is not going to give you any nourishment. Forget the finger and look at where it is pointing.

The Masters illuminate. They shower great light—

they are light—they shower great light on your being. They are like a searchlight: they focus their being on your being. You have lived in darkness for centuries, for millions of lives. Suddenly a Master's searchlight starts revealing a few forgotten territories in you. They are within you; the Master is not bringing them—he is simply bringing his light, he is focussing himself on you. And the Master can focus only when the disciple is open, when the disciple is surrendered, when the disciple is ready to learn, not to argue, when the disciple has come not to accumulate knowledge but to know truth, when the disciple is not only curious but is a seeker and is ready to risk all. Even if life has to be risked and sacrificed the disciple is ready. In fact, when you risk your sleepy life, you sacrifice your sleepy life, you attain to a totally different quality of life: the life of light, of love, the life which is beyond death, beyond time, beyond change.

They illuminate and confirm realization. First the Master illuminates the way, the truth that is within you. And secondly: when you realize it, when you recognize it. . . . It is very difficult for you to believe that you have attained it. The most unbelievable thing is when realization of truth happens to you, because you have been told that it is very difficult, almost impossible, and that it takes millions of lives to arrive at it. And you have been told it is somewhere else—maybe in heaven—and when you recognize it within yourself, how can you believe it?

The Master confirms it. He says, "Yes, this is it!" His confirmation is as much needed as his illumination. He begins by illuminating and ends by confirming. The Masters are evidence of truth, not its proof.

Meditate over the subtle difference between evidence and proof. The Master is an evidence; he is a witness. He has seen, he has known, he has become. You can feel it; the evidence can be felt. You can come closer and closer; you can allow the fragrance of the Master to penetrate to the innermost core of your being. The Master is only evidence; he is not proof. If you want any proof. . . there is no proof.

God can neither be proved nor disproved; it is not an argument. God is not a hypothesis, it is not a theory: it is experience. The Master is living evidence. But to see it you will need a different approach than you are accustomed to.

You know how to approach a teacher, how to approach a professor, how to approach a priest. They don't require much because they simply impart information which can be done even by a tape recorder or by a computer or by a gramophone record or by a book.

I WAS A STUDENT IN A UNIVERSITY. I never attended the classes of my professors. Naturally, they were offended. And one day the head of the department called me and he said, "Why have you joined the university? We never see you, you never attend any classes. And remember: when the examination time comes, don't ask for an attendance record—because seventy-five percent attendance is a must to enter into the examination."

I took hold of the hand of that old man and I said, "You come with me—I will show you where I am and why I have entered the university."

He was a little afraid of where I was taking him and why. And it was a well-known fact that I was a little eccentric! He said, "But where are you taking me?"

I said, "I will show you that you have to give me one hundred percent attendance. You come with me."

I took him to the library and I told the librarian, "You tell this old man—has there ever been a single day when I have not been in the library?"

The librarian said, "Even on holidays he has been here. If the library is not open then this student goes on sitting in the garden of the library, but he comes. And every day we have to tell him, 'Now please, you leave, because it is closing time.' "

I told the professor, "I find the books far more clear than your so-called professors. And, moreover, they simply repeat what is already written in the books, so what is the point of going on listening to them second-hand? I can look in the books directly!"

I told him, "If you can prove that your teachers are teaching something which is not in the books, then I am ready to come to the classes. If you cannot prove it, then keep it in mind that you have to give me one hundred percent attendance—otherwise I will create trouble!"

And I never went to ask him; he gave me one hundred percent attendance. He followed the point; it was so simple. He said, "You are right. Why listen to second-hand knowledge? You can go directly to the books. I know those professors—I myself am just a gramophone record. The truth is," he said to me, "that for thirty years I have not read anything. I just go on using my old notes."

For thirty years he has been teaching the same thing again and again and again; and in thirty years' time, millions of books have been published.

You know how to approach a teacher, you know

how to approach a book, you know how to approach dead information, but you don't know how to approach a Master. It is a totally different way of communing. It is not communication, it is communion—because the Master is not a proof but an evidence. He is not an argument for God, he is a witness for God. He does not possess great knowledge *about* God, he knows. He is not knowledgeable, he simply knows.

Remember, to know *about* is worthless. The word "about" means around. To know about something means to go on moving in circles, around and around. The word "about" is beautiful. Whenever you read "about," read "around." When somebody says, "I know *about* God," read: he knows *around* God. He goes in a circle. And real knowing is never about, never around; it is direct, it is a straight line.

Jesus says: "Straight is the path. . . ." It does not go in circles; it is a jump from the periphery to the center. The Master is an evidence of that jump, that quantum leap, that transformation.

You have to approach the Master with great love, with great trust, with an open heart. You are not aware who you are. He is aware who he is, he is aware who you are. The caterpillar might be said to be unaware that it may become a butterfly. You are caterpillars—*bodhisattvas.* All caterpillars are *bodhisattvas* and all *bodhisattvas* are caterpillars. A *bodhisattva* means one who can become a butterfly, who can become a Buddha, who *is* a Buddha in the seed, in essence. But how can the caterpillar be aware that he can become a butterfly? The only way is to commune with butterflies, to see butterflies moving in the wind, in the sun. Seeing them soaring high, seeing them moving from one flower to another flower, seeing their beauty, their color, maybe a deep desire, a longing arises in the caterpillar: "Can I also be the same?" In that very moment the caterpillar has started awakening, a process has been triggered.

The Master/disciple relationship is the relationship between a caterpillar and a butterfly, a friendship between a caterpillar and a butterfly. The butterfly cannot prove that the caterpillar can become a butterfly; there is no logical way. But the butterfly can provoke a longing in the caterpillar—that is possible.

The Master helps you to reach your own experience. He does not give you the Vedas, the Koran, the Bible; he throws you to yourself. He makes you aware of your inner sources. He makes you aware of your own juice, of your own godliness. He liberates you from the scriptures. He liberates you from the interpretations of others. He liberates you from all belief. He liberates you from all speculation, from all guesswork. He liberates you from philosophy and from religion and from theology. He liberates you, in short, from the world of words—because the word is the problem.

You become so much obsessed with the word "love" that you forget that love is an experience, not a word. You become so obsessed with the word "God" that you forget that God is an experience, not a word. The word "God" is not God, and the word "fire" is not fire, and the word "love" is not love either.

The Master liberates you from words, he liberates you from all kinds of imaginative philosophies. He brings you to a state of wordless silence. The failure of religion and philosophy is that they all become substitutes for real experience. Beware of it!

Marlene and Florence, two Denver secretaries, were chatting over lunch.

"I was raped last night by a scholar," whispered Marlene.

"Really?" said Florence. "How did you know he was a scholar?"

"I had to help him."

Scholars are crippled people, paralyzed, hung up in their heads. They have forgotten everything except words. They are great system-makers. They accumulate beautiful theories; they arrange them in beautiful patterns, but that's all they do. They know nothing— although they deceive others and deceive themselves, too, that they know.

A man went into a restaurant to have some lunch and when the waiter came he said, "I will have a plate of kiddlies, please."

"What?" said the waiter.

"Kiddlies," said the man.

"What?" said the waiter again.

So the man picked up the menu and pointed at what he wanted. "Kiddlies," he repeated firmly.

"Ah," said the waiter. "I see. Kidneys. Why didn't you say so?"

"But," said the man, "I said kiddlies, diddle I?"

It is very difficult to pull them out. They live in their own words. They have forgotten that reality has anything else in it but words. They are utterly deaf, utterly blind. They can't see, they can't hear, they can't feel. Words are words. You can't see them, you can't feel them, but they can give you great ego.

A cannibal rushed into his village to spread the

word that a hunting party had captured a Christian theologian.

"Good," said one of the cannibals enthusiastically,
"I have always wanted to try a baloney sandwich."

Beware of getting lost in philosophy and religion if
you really want to know what truth is. Beware of being
Christian, Hindu, Mohammedan, because they are all
ways of being deaf, blind, insensitive.

Three deaf British gentlemen were traveling on a
train bound for London.

The first said, "Pardon me, conductor, what station
is this?"

"Wembley, sir," answered the conductor.

"Good Lord!" exclaimed the second Englishman. "I
am sure it is Thursday."

"So am I," agreed the third. "Let us all go into the
bar car and have a drink."

That's how it goes on between professors,
philosophers, theologians. They can't hear what is being said. They have their own ideas and they are so full
of them, so many thick layers of words, that reality cannot reach them.

ZEN SAYS: IF YOU CAN DROP PHILOSOPHIZING, there is
a hope for you. The moment you drop philosophizing you become innocent like a child. But remember: the Zen emphasis on not knowing does not mean
that it emphasizes ignorance. Not knowing is not ignorance; not knowing is a state of innocence. There is
neither knowledge nor ignorance; both have been
transcended.

An ignorant man is one who ignores; that's how the

word comes. The root is "ignoring." The ignorant person is one who goes on ignoring something essential. In that way the knowledgeable person is the most ignorant person, because he knows about heaven and hell and he knows nothing about himself. He knows about God, but he knows nothing about who he is, what this consciousness inside is. He is ignorant because he is ignoring the *most* fundamental thing in life: he is ignoring himself. He is keeping himself occupied with the non-essential. He is ignorant—full of knowledge, yet utterly ignorant.

Not knowing simply means a state of no-mind. Mind can be knowledgeable, mind can be ignorant. If you have little information you will be thought ignorant; if you have more information you will be thought knowledgeable. Between ignorance and knowledge the difference is that of quantity, of degrees. The ignorant person is less knowledgeable, that's all; the very knowledgeable person may appear to the world as less ignorant, but they are not different, their qualities are not different.

Zen emphasizes the state of not knowing. Not knowing means one is neither ignorant nor knowledgeable. One is not knowledgeable because one is not interested in mere information, and one is not ignorant because one is not ignoring—one is not ignoring the most essential quest. One is not ignoring one's own being, one's own consciousness.

Not knowing has a beauty of its own, a purity. It is just like a pure mirror, a lake utterly silent, reflecting the stars and the trees on the bank. The state of not knowing is the highest point in man's evolution.

Knowledge is introduced to the mind after physical birth. Knowing is always present, like the heart knowing how to beat or a seed knowing how to sprout, or a flower knowing how to grow, or a fish knowing how to swim. And it is quite different from knowing about things. So please make a distinction between knowledge and knowing.

The state of not knowing is really the state of knowing because when all knowledge and all ignorance have disappeared you can reflect existence as it is. Knowledge is acquired after your birth, but knowing comes with you. And the more knowledge you acquire, the more and more knowing starts disappearing because it becomes covered with knowledge. Knowledge is exactly like dust and knowing is like a mirror.

The heart of knowing is now. Knowledge is always of the past. Knowledge means memory. Knowledge means you have known something, you have experienced something, and you have accumulated your experience. Knowing is of the present. And how can you be in the present if you are clinging too much to knowledge? That is impossible; you will have to drop clinging to knowledge. And knowledge is acquired: knowing is your nature. Knowing is always now—the heart of knowing is now. And the heart of now...?

The word "now" is beautiful. The heart of it is the letter "O" which is also a symbol for zero. The heart of now is zero, nothingness. When the mind is no more, when you are just a nothingness, just a zero—Buddha calls it exactly that, *shunya,* the zero—then everything that surrounds you, *all* that is within and without, is known, but known not as knowledge, known in a totally different way. The same way that the flower knows how to open, and the fish knows how to swim, and the child knows in the mother's womb how to grow, and you know how to breathe—even while asleep, even in a coma, you go on breathing—and the heart knows how to beat. This is a totally different kind of knowing, so intrinsic, so internal. It is not acquired, it is natural.

Knowledge is got in exchange for knowing. And when you have got knowledge, what happens to knowing? You forget knowing. You have got knowledge and you have forgotten knowing. And knowing is the door to the divine; knowledge is a barrier to the divine. Knowledge has utility in the world. Yes, it will make you more efficient, skillful, a good mechanic, this and that; you may be able to earn in a better way. All that is there and I am not denying it. And you can use knowledge in that way; but don't let knowledge become a barrier to the divine. Whenever knowledge is not needed, put it aside and drown yourself into a state of not knowing—which is also a state of knowing, real knowing. Knowledge is got in exchange for knowing and knowing is *for*gotten. It has only to be *re*membered—you have forgotten it.

The function of the Master is to help you *re*-member it. The mind has to be *re*-minded, for knowing is nothing but *re*-cognition, *re*-collection, *re*-membrance. When you come across some truth, when you come across a Master, and you see the truth of his being, something within you immediately recognizes it. Not even a single moment is lost. You don't think about it, whether it is true or not—thinking needs time. When you listen to the truth, when you feel the presence of truth, when you come into close communion with the truth, something within you immediately recognizes it, with no argumentation. Not that you accept, not that you believe: you recognize. And it could not be recognized if it were not already known somehow, somewhere, deep down within you.

This is the fundamental approach of Zen.

"Has your baby brother learned to talk yet?"

"Oh, sure," replied little Mike. "Now Mummy and Daddy are teaching him to keep quiet."

The society teaches you knowledge. So many schools, colleges, universities . . . they are all devoted to creating knowledge, more knowledge, implanting knowledge in people. And the function of the Master is just the opposite: what your society has done to you the Master has to undo. His function is basically anti-social, and nothing can be done about it. The Master is bound to be anti-social.

Jesus, Pythagoras, Buddha, Lao Tzu, they are all anti-social. Not that they want to be anti-social, but the moment they recognize the beauty of not knowing, the vastness of not knowing, the innocence of not knowing, the moment the taste of not knowing happens to them, they want to impart it to others, they want to share it with others. And that very process is anti-social.

People ask me why the society is against me. The society is *not* against me—*I* am anti-social. But I can't help it—I have to do my thing. I have to share what has happened to me, and in that very sharing I go against the society. Its whole structure is rooted in knowledge, and the Master's function is to destroy both knowledge and ignorance and to bring you back your childhood.

Jesus says: Unless you are like small children you will not enter into the kingdom of God.

The society, in fact, makes you uprooted from your nature. It pushes you off your center. It makes you neurotic.

Conducting a university course, a famous psychiatrist was asked by a student, "Sir, you have told us about the abnormal person and his behavior, but what about the normal person?"

"When we find him," replied the psychiatrist, "we cure him."

The society goes on curing normal people. Every child is born normal, remember; then the society cures him. Then he becomes abnormal. He becomes Hindu, Mohammedan, Christian, Communist, Catholic . . . there are so many kinds of neurosis in the world. You can choose, you can shop for whatever kind of neurosis you want. Society creates all kinds; all sizes and shapes of neurosis are available, to everybody's liking.

Zen cures you of your abnormality. It makes you again normal, it makes you again ordinary. It does not make you a saint, remember. It does not make you a holy person, remember. It simply makes you an ordinary person—takes you back to your nature, back to your source.

This beautiful anecdote:

Ascending to the high seat, Dogen Zenji said:
"Zen Master Hogen studied with Keishin Zenji.

Once Keishin Zenji asked him,
'Joza, where do you go?'

Hogen said, 'I am making pilgrimage aimlessly.'

Keishin said, 'What is the matter of your pilgrimage?'

Hogen said, 'I don't know.'

Keishin said, 'Not knowing is the most intimate.'

Hogen suddenly attained great enlightenment."

NOW MEDITATE OVER EACH WORD of this small anecdote; it contains all the great scriptures of the world. It contains more than all the great scriptures contain—because it also contains not knowing.

Ascending to the high seat . . .

This is just a symbolic, metaphorical way of saying something very significant. Zen says that man is a ladder. The lowest rung is the mind and the highest rung of the ladder is the no-mind. Zen says only people who have attained to no-mind are worthy enough to ascend to the high seat and speak to people—not everybody. It is not a question of a priest or a preacher.

Christians train preachers; they have theological colleges where preachers are trained. What kind of foolishness is this? Yes, you can teach them the art of eloquence; you can teach them how to begin a speech, how to end a speech. And that's exactly what is being taught in Christian theological colleges. Even what gestures to make, when to make a pause, when to speak slowly and when to become loud—everything is cultivated. And these stupid people go on preaching about Jesus, and they have not asked a single question!

Once I visited a theological college. The principal was my friend; he invited me. I asked him, "Can you tell me in what theological college Jesus learned?—because the Sermon on the Mount is so beautiful, he must have learned in some theological college. In what theological college did Buddha learn?"

Mohammed was absolutely uneducated, but the way he speaks, the way he sings in the Koran, is superb. It is coming from somewhere else. It is not education, it is not knowledge. It is coming from a state of no-mind.

Little Johnny was the son of the local minister. One day his teacher was asking the class what they wanted to be when they grew up.

When it was his turn to answer he replied, "I want to be a minister just like my father."

The teacher was impressed with his determination and so she asked him why he wanted to be a preacher.

"Well," he said thoughtfully, "since I have to go to church on Sunday anyway, I figure it would be more interesting to be the guy who stands up and yells than the one who has to sit down and listen."

You can create preachers, but you cannot create Masters.

In India, the seat from where a Master speaks is called *vyaspeetha*. Vyasa was one of the greatest Masters India has ever produced, one of the ancient-most Buddhas. He was so influential, his impact was so tremendous, that thousands of books exist in his name which were not written by him. But his name became so important that anybody who wanted to sell his book would put Vyasa's name on it instead of putting his own name. His name was guarantee enough that the book was valuable. Now scholars go crazy deciding which is the real book written by Vyasa.

The seat from where a Buddha speaks is called *vyaspeetha*—the seat of the Buddha. Nobody else is allowed to ascend to the seat unless he has attained to no-mind. *Ascending to the high seat* is a metaphor: it says the man has attained to the state of no-mind, he has attained the state of not-knowing which is true knowing.

> ... *Dogen Zenji said:*
> "*Zen Master Hogen studied with Keishin Zenji.*

Once Keishin Zenji asked him,
'Joza, where do you go?' "

This is a Zen way of saying, "What is your goal in life? Where are you going?" It also implies another question: "From where are you coming? What is the source of your life?" It also implies, "Who are you?"—because if you can answer where you are coming from and where you are going to, that means you must know who you are.

The three most important questions are: "Who am I? From where do I come? And to where am I going?"

. . . Keishin Zenji asked
"Joza, where do you go?"

Hogen said, "I am making pilgrimage aimlessly."

See the beauty of the answer. This is how tremendously beautiful things transpire between a Master and a disciple. He said:

"I am making pilgrimage aimlessly."

If you are going to Kaaba, then it is not a pilgrimage because there is an aim in it; if you are going to Jerusalem or to Kashi it is not a pilgrimage. Wherever there is a goal there is ambition, and wherever there is ambition there is mind, desire. And with desire there is no possibility of any pilgrimage.

A pilgrimage can only be aimless. See the beauty of it! Only a Zen Master can approve it and only a Zen disciple can say something so tremendously revolutionary.

"I am making pilgrimage aimlessly."

The Master asks, "Where are you going?" And the disciple says, "Nowhere in particular." Aimlessly, just like a dry leaf in the wind, wherever the wind takes it: to the north, then the north is beautiful; to the south, then the south is beautiful—because all is divine. Wherever you go you encounter him. There is no need to have any aim.

The moment you have any aim you become tense; you become concentrated on the aim. The moment you have any aim you are separate from the whole. You have a private goal, and to have a private goal is the root of all ego. Not to have a private goal is to be one with the whole, and to be one with the whole is possible only if you are aimlessly wandering.

A Zen person is a wanderer, aimless, with no goal, with no future. Moment-to-moment he lives without any mind; just like the dry leaf he makes himself available to the winds. He says to the winds, "Take me wherever you want." If he rises on the winds high in the sky he does not feel superior to others who are lying down on the ground. If he falls to the ground he does not feel inferior to others who are rising on the wind high in the sky. He cannot fail. He cannot ever be frustrated. When there is no goal, how can you fail? And when you are not going anywhere in particular, how can you be in frustration? Expectation brings frustration. Private ambitions bring failures.

The Zen person is always victorious, even in his failure.

> *Keishin said, "What is the matter of your pilgrimage?"*

He asks again to make certain, because he may be simply repeating. He may have read in some old Zen scriptures that "One should be aimless. When one is aimless, life is a pilgrimage." Hence the Master asks again:

... *"What is the matter of your pilgrimage?"*

Hogen said, "I don't know."

Now, if Hogen was only repeating some knowledge gathered from scriptures or others, he would have again answered the same thing, maybe paraphrased in a different way. He would have been like a parrot. The Master is asking the same question, but the answer has changed, totally changed. He simply says: *I don't know.*

How can you know if you are aimless? How can you know when you don't have any goal? How can you be when there is no goal? The ego can exist only with goals, ambitions, desires.

Hogen said, "I don't know."

His answer, his response, is not parrotlike. He has not repeated the same thing again. The question was the same, remember, but the answer has changed. That's the difference between a knowledgeable person and a man of knowing, the wise man, who functions out of a state of not-knowing.

"I don't know."

Keishin must have been tremendously happy. He said:

"Not knowing is the most intimate."

Knowledge creates a distance between you and reality. The more you know, the greater is the distance—so many books between you and reality. If you have crammed the whole of the *Encyclopaedia Britannica*, then there is so much distance between you and reality. Unless reality tries to find you through the jungle of the *Encyclopaedia Britannica* or you try to find reality through the jungle of the *Encyclopaedia Britannica*, there is not going to be any meeting. The more you know, the greater is the distance; the less you know, the thinner is the distance. If you don't know at all there is no distance at all. Then you are face to face with reality; not even face to face—*you are it.* That's why the Master said:

> *"Not knowing is the most intimate."*

Remember, such a beautiful sutra, so exquisite, so tremendously significant:

> *"Not knowing is the most intimate."*

The moment you don't know, intimacy arises between you and reality, a great friendship arises. It becomes a love affair. You are embracing reality; reality penetrates you, as lovers penetrate each other. You melt into it like snow melting in the sun. You become one with it. There is nothing to divide. It is knowledge that divides; it is not-knowing that unites.

Listening to this tremendously significant sutra:

> *"Not knowing is the most intimate,"*
> *Hogen suddenly attained great enlightenment.*

H E MUST HAVE BEEN VERY CLOSE, obviously. When he said, *"I don't know,"* he must have been just on the borderline. When he said, *"I am making pilgrimage aimlessly,"* he was just one step away from the borderline. When he said, *"I don't know,"* even that one step disappeared. He was standing on the borderline.

And when the Master said, when the Master confirmed, illuminated, and said, *"Not knowing is the most intimate"*. . . . when the Master patted him on the back: *"Not knowing is the most intimate"*. . . .

Hogen suddenly attained great enlightenment.

Immediately, that very moment, he crossed the border. Immediately his last clinging disappeared. Now he cannot even say, "I don't know."

The stupid person says, "I know"; the intelligent person comes to know that "I don't know." But there is a transcendence of both when only silence prevails. Nothing can be said, nothing can be uttered. Hogen entered that silence, that great enlightenment, and suddenly, immediately, without any lapse of time.

Enlightenment is always sudden because it is not an achievement; it is already the case. It is only a remembering, it is only a reminding, it is only a recognition. You are already enlightened; you are just not aware of it. It is awareness of that which is already the case.

Meditate over this beautiful anecdote. Let this sutra resound in your being:

"Not knowing is the most intimate."

And one never knows: sudden enlightenment may happen to you as it happened to Hogen. It is going to happen to many people here, because what I am doing every day is destroying your knowledge, destroying and destroying all your clingings and strategies of the mind. Any day when your mind collapses, when you cannot hold it together any more, there is bound to be sudden enlightenment. It is not an attainment, hence it can happen in a single moment, instantly. Society has forced you to forget it; my work here is to help you remember it.

All the teachings the sages expounded are no more than commentaries on your sudden cry: "Ah, this!"

Neti
Neti

The first question

Bhagwan,
Please, in the question "Who am I?"
what does "I" mean? Does it mean the
essence of life?

Hermann Sander,

WHO AM I?" IS NOT REALLY A QUESTION because it has no answer to it; it is unanswerable. It is a device, not a question. It is used as a mantra. When you constantly enquire inside, "Who am I? Who am I?" you are not waiting for an answer. Your mind will supply many answers; all those answers have to be rejected. Your mind will say, "You are the essence of life. You are the eternal soul. You are divine," and so on and so forth. All those answers have to be rejected: *neti neti*—one has to go on saying, "Neither this nor that."

When you have denied all the possible answers that

the mind can supply and devise, when the question remains absolutely unanswerable, a miracle happens: suddenly the question also disappears. When all the answers have been rejected, the question has no props, no supports inside to stand on any more. It simply flops, it collapses, it disappears.

When the question also has disappeared, then you know. But that knowing is not an answer: it is an existential experience. Nothing can be said about it, or whatever will be said will be wrong. To say anything about it is to falsify it. It is the ultimate mystery, inexpressible, indefinable. No word is adequate enough to describe it. Even the phrase "essence of life" is not adequate; even "God" is not adequate. Nothing is adequate to express it; its very nature is inexpressible.

But you know. You know exactly the way the seed knows how to grow—not like the professor who knows about chemistry or physics or geography or history, but like the bud which knows how to open in the early morning sun. Not like the priest who knows about God; about and about he goes, around and around he goes.

Knowledge is beating around the bush: knowing is a direct penetration. But the moment you directly penetrate into existence, you disappear as a separate entity. You are no more. When the *knower* is no more then the knowing is. And the knowing is not *about* something—you are that knowing itself.

So *I* cannot say, Sander, what "I" means in the question "Who am I?" It means nothing! It is just a device to lead you into the unknown, to lead you into the uncharted, to lead you into that which is not available to the mind. It is a sword to cut the very roots of the mind, so only the silence of no-mind is left. In that silence there is no question, no answer, no knower, no known, but only knowing, only experiencing.

That's why the mystics appear to be in such difficulty to express it. Many of them have remained silent out of the awareness that whatsoever you say goes wrong; the moment you say it, it goes wrong. Those who have spoken, they have spoken with the condition: "Don't cling to our words."

Lao Tzu says: "Tao, once described, is no more the real Tao." The moment you say something about it you have already falsified it, you have betrayed it. It is such an intimate knowing, incommunicable.

"Who am I?" functions like a sword to cut all the answers that the mind can manage. Zen people will say it is a koan, just like other koans. There are many koans, famous koans. One is: "Find out your original face." And the disciple asks the Master, "What is the original face?" And the Master says, "The face that you had before your parents were born."

And you start meditating on that: "What is your original face?" Naturally, you have to deny all your faces. Many faces will start surfacing: childhood faces, when you were young, when you became middle-aged, when you became old, when you were healthy, when you were ill. . . . All kinds of faces will stand in a queue. They will pass before your eyes claiming, "I am the original face." And you have to go on rejecting.

When all the faces have been rejected and emptiness is left, you have found the original face. Emptiness is the original face. Zero is the ultimate experience. Nothingness—or more accurately *no-thingness*—is your original face.

Or another famous koan is: "The sound of one hand clapping." The Master says to the disciple, "Go and listen to the sound of one hand clapping." Now this is patent absurdity: one hand cannot clap and without clapping there can be no sound. The Master knows it, the disciple knows it. But when the Master says, "Go and meditate on it," the disciple has to follow.

He starts making efforts to listen to the sound of one hand clapping. Many sounds come to his mind: the birds singing, the sound of running water. . . . He rushes immediately to the Master; he says, "I have heard it! The sound of running water—isn't that the sound of one hand clapping?"

And the Master hits him hard on the head and he says, "You fool! Go back, meditate more!"

And he goes on meditating, and the mind goes on providing new answers: "The sound of wind passing through the pine trees—certainly this is the answer." He is in such a hurry! Everybody is in such a hurry. Impatiently he rushes to the door of the Master, a little bit apprehensive, afraid too, but maybe this is the answer. . . .

And even before he has said a single thing the Master hits him! He is very much puzzled and he says, "This is too much! I have not even uttered a single word, so how can I be wrong? And why are you hitting me?"

The Master says, "It is not a question of whether you have uttered something or not. You have come with an answer—that is enough proof that you must be wrong. When you have *really* found it you won't come; there will be no need. *I* will come to you."

Sometimes years pass, and then one day it has happened, there is no answer. First the disciple knew that there was no answer to it, but it was only an intellectual knowing. Now he knows from his very core: "There is no answer!" All answers have evaporated.

And the sure sign that all answers have evaporated is only one: when the question also evaporates. Now he is sitting silently doing nothing, not even meditating. He has forgotten the question: "What is the sound of one hand clapping?" It is no more there. It is *pure* silence.

And there are ways . . . there are inner paths which exist between a Master and a disciple. And now the Master rushes towards the disciple. He knocks on his door. He hugs the disciple and says, "So it has happened? This is it! No answer, no question: this is it. Ah, this!"

The second question

Bhagwan,
I feel life is very boring. What
should I do?

Brij Mohan,

AS IT IS, YOU HAVE ALREADY DONE ENOUGH. You have made life boring—some achievement! Life is such a dance of ecstasy and you have reduced it to boredom. You have done a miracle! What else do you want to do? You can't do anything bigger than this. Life and boring? You must have a tremendous capacity to *ignore* life.

Just the other day I was telling you that ignorance means the capacity to ignore. You must be ignoring the birds, the trees, the flowers, the people. Otherwise, life is so tremendously beautiful, so *absurdly* beautiful, that if you can see it as it is you will never stop laughing. You will go on giggling—at least inside.

Life is not boring, but *mind* is boring. And we create such a mind, such a strong mind, like a China Wall around ourselves, that it does not allow life to enter into us. It disconnects us from life. We become isolated, encapsulated, windowless. Living behind a prison wall you don't see the morning sun, you don't see the birds on the wing, you don't see the sky in the night full of stars. And, of course, you start thinking that life is boring. Your conclusion is wrong. *You* are in a wrong space; you are living in a wrong context.

You must be a religious person, Brij Mohan, because to make life boring one has to be religious; one has to be very scholarly. One has to know Christianity, Hinduism, Islam. One has to learn much from the Vedas and the Koran and the Bible. You must be very well-informed. A man who is too well-informed, too knowledgeable, creates such a thick wall of words— futile words, empty words—around himself that he becomes incapable of seeing life.

Knowledge is a barrier to life.

Put aside your knowledge! And then look with empty eyes . . . and life is a *constant* surprise. And I am not talking about some divine life—the *ordinary* life is so extraordinary. In small incidents you will find the presence of God—a child giggling, a dog barking, a peacock dancing. But you can't see if your eyes are covered with knowledge. The poorest man in the world is the man who lives behind a curtain of knowledge.

The poorest are those who live through the mind.

The richest are those who have opened the windows of no-mind and approached life with the no-mind.

Brij Mohan, this is not only *your* experience; you are not alone in it. In fact, the majority of people will agree with you. They don't find any surprise anywhere. And each moment there are surprises and surprises because life is never the same; it is constantly changing, and it takes such unpredictable turns. How can you remain unaffected by the very wonder of it? The only way to remain unaffected is to cling to your past, to your experience, to your knowledge, to your memories, to your mind. Then you cannot see that which is; you go on missing the present.

Miss the present and you live in boredom. *Be* in the present and you will be surprised that there is no boredom at all. Start by looking around a little more like a child. Be a child again! That's what meditation is all about: being a child again—a rebirth, being innocent again, not-knowing. That's what we were saying the other day. The Master said: *Not-knowing is the most intimate.*

Yes, you must have become very alienated from life, hence boredom. You have forgotten the intimacy, the immediacy. You are no longer bridged. Knowledge functions as a wall: innocence functions as a bridge.

Start looking like a child again. Go to the seashore and again start collecting seashells. See a child collecting seashells—as if he has found a mine of diamonds. So thrilled he is! See a child making sandcastles and how absorbed he is, utterly lost, as if there is nothing more important than making sandcastles. See a child running after a butterfly . . . and be a child again. Start running after butterflies again. Make sandcastles, collect seashells.

Don't live as if you know. You know nothing! All that you know is about and about. The moment you *know* something, boredom disappears. Knowing is such an adventure that boredom cannot exist. With knowledge of course it can exist; with knowing it cannot exist.

And let me remind you: I am not talking about some divine knowledge, some esoteric knowledge; I am simply talking about *this* life. Just look around with a little more clarity, with a little more transparency . . . and life is hilarious!

A downtown store featured a plaque in its window reading: BUY AMERICAN. Printed in small letters at the bottom was: *MADE IN JAPAN*.

Just start looking around a little more carefully.

A German in the Soviet Zone reported to the police that his parrot was missing. He was asked whether the parrot talked.

"Yes," he replied, "but any political opinions he expresses are strictly his own."

Molly, aged seventy-nine, complained of abdominal swelling and pain to the doctor. He examined her thoroughly, put her through a series of laboratory tests, and then announced the results.

"The plain fact, madam," said the medical man, "is that you are pregnant."

"That's impossible!" said Molly. "Why, I am seventy-nine years old and my husband, although he still works, is eighty-six!"

The doctor insisted, so the aging mother-to-be pulled over his desk telephone and dialed her husband's office. When he was on the line she shouted,

"You old goat, you have got me pregnant!"

"Please," quavered the old man, "who did you say was calling?"

The third question

Bhagwan,
I know you want us all to rid ourselves
of our egos and minds, and in my case, I
know that this is very necessary, but for
those of us who will be returning to the
West, would not a total absence of mind or
ego make life much more difficult?

Prem Joyce,

WHEN I SAY, "DROP THE EGO, DROP THE MIND," I don't mean that you cannot use the mind any more. In fact, when you don't cling to the mind you can use it in a far better, far more efficient way, because the energy that was involved in clinging becomes available. And when you are not continuously in the mind, twenty-four hours a day in the mind, the mind also gets a little time to rest.

Do you know?—even metals need rest, even metals get tired. So what to say about this subtle mechanism of the mind? It is the *most* subtle mechanism in the world. In such a small skull you are carrying such a complicated biocomputer that no computer made by man is yet capable of competing with it. The scientists say a single man's brain can contain all the libraries of the world and yet there will be space enough to contain more.

And you are continuously using it—uselessly, unnecessarily! You have forgotten how to put it off. For seventy, eighty years it remains on, working, working, tired. That's why people lose intelligence: for the simple reason that they are so tired. If the mind can have a little rest, if you can leave the mind alone for a few hours every day, if once in a while you can give the mind a holiday, it will be rejuvenated; it will come out more intelligent, more efficient, more skillful.

So I am *not* saying that you are *not* to use your mind, but don't be *used* by the mind. Right now the mind is the master and you are only a slave.

Meditation makes you a master and the mind becomes a slave. And remember: the mind as a master is dangerous because, after all, it is a machine; but the mind as a slave is tremendously significant, useful. A machine should function as a machine, not as a master. Our priorities are all upside-down—your *consciousness* should be the master.

So whenever you want to use it, in the East or in the West—of course you will need it in the marketplace—*use* it! But when you don't need it, when you are resting at home by the side of your swimming-pool or in your garden, there is no need. Put it aside. Forget all about it! Then just be.

And the same is the case with the ego. Don't be identified with it, that's all. Remember that you are part of the whole; you are not separate from it.

That does not mean that if somebody is stealing from your house you have simply to watch—because you are just part of the whole and he is also part of the whole, so what is wrong? And somebody is taking money from your pocket, so there is no problem—the other's hand is as much yours as his! I am not saying that.

Remember that you are part of the whole so that you can relax, merge; once in a while you can be utterly drowned in the whole. And that will give you a new lease of life. The inexhaustible sources of the whole will become available to you. You will come out of it refreshed; you will come out of it reborn, again as a child, full of joy, enquiry, adventure, ecstasy.

Don't get identified with the ego, although, as far as the world is concerned, you have to function as an ego—that is only utilitarian! You have to use the word "I"—use the word "I," but remember that it is only a word. It has a certain utility, and without it life will become impossible. If you stop using the word "I" completely, life will become impossible. We know names are only utilitarian, nobody is born with a name. But I am not saying to drop the name and throw your passport into the river. Then you will be in trouble! You *need* a name; that is a necessity because you live with so many people.

If you are alone in the world, then of course there is no need to carry a passport. If you are alone . . . for example, if the third world war happens and Joyce is left alone, then there will be no need to carry a passport; you can throw it anywhere. Then there will be no need to have any name. Even if you have one it will be useless—nobody will ever call you. Then there will be no need to even use the word "I" because "I" needs a "thou"; without a "thou" the "I" is meaningless. It has meaning only in the context of others.

So don't misunderstand me. *Use* your ego, but use it just like you use your shoes and your umbrella and your clothes. When it is raining, use the umbrella, but don't go on carrying it unnecessarily. And don't go to bed with the umbrella, and don't be afraid that in a dream it may rain. . . . The umbrella has a utility, so use it when it is needed; but don't become so identified with the umbrella that you cannot put it aside. Use the shoes, use the clothes, use the name—they are all utilities, not realities.

In the world, when so many people are there, we need a few labels, a few symbols, just to demark, just to make sure who is who.

You ask me: *I know you want us all to rid ourselves of our egos and minds . . . .*

I am not saying to "get rid"; I am simply saying to be master of your minds. I am not telling you to be mindless; I am only saying: don't just be minds—you are far more. Be consciousnesses! Then the mind becomes a small thing. You can use it whenever needed, and whenever not needed you can put it off.

I am using my mind when I am talking to you. The mind has to be used; there is no other way. But the moment I enter my room, then I don't go on using it—there is no point. Then I am simply silent. With you I am using the language, the words, but when I am with myself there is no need for any language, for any words. When I am settled into myself and there is no question of communication, language disappears. Then there is a totally different kind of consciousness.

Right now my consciousness is flowing through the mind, using the mechanism of the mind to approach you. I can reach for you with my hand, but I am not the hand. And when I touch you with my hand, the hand is only a means; something else is touching you through the hand.

The body has to be used, the mind has to be used, the ego, the language, and all kinds of things have to be used. And you are allowed to use them with only one condition: remain the master.

The fourth question

Bhagwan,
The other day you answered my question
about loving three women. A few things have
happened since then. In the first place, I
missed you because I was not in the discourse
but in the arms of the chosen one, which
turned out to be a bad choice because she ran
straight away and into the arms of somebody
else after she realized that she was chosen.
Then, in spite of this, the little commune
has grown into five women now. One woman
is hell, but what to say about five? But I
have got a little help from my friends. For
instance, Hamid has suggested I turn gay
and has offered me a date with him. Vivek
suggested that I wait until there are seven.
But please, Bhagwan, before I disappear into
the seventh hell, I have already lost three
kilos in weight. You offered to buy me out.
Can't we talk business now? I really mean it!

Prem Aditya,

A PREACHER WAS LISTENING to a young man confess his sins. In the middle of it he stopped him. "Wait a minute, young man," he said, "you ain't confessin' —you are braggin'."

Now you have started bragging! I know perfectly well ... because I am in contact with your three women too. I also mean business! You don't have five —you have even lost the three. And today you are here because there is nobody you can be with!
Hamid is generous ... but, remember, he is an Iranian!

One day, back when the draft was still in effect, Glascox received his induction notice. He reported to his draft board and confessed that he was a homosexual.
"Queer, huh?" one member grunted. "Do you think you could kill a man?"
"Oh, yes," giggled Glascox, "but it would take me quite a while!"

And let me make you aware that before you can kill an Iranian the Iranian will kill you! So avoid Hamid— he is generous, but avoid him! He is also tired of women. He has just separated from Divya, so he must be feeling lonely.
And Vivek's suggestion is very esoteric. She is becoming a little esoteric, by and by. Being the chief medium she has many esoteric mediums under her so she is learning a few esoteric numbers. Seven is really dangerous!
And your guess is right: seven women will lead you

to the seventh hell. And that is the last, the rock bottom; you cannot fall below that. Vivek must have suggested it so that once you have fallen to the rock bottom you start rising back up because there is nowhere else to go.

And you say you have lost three kilos in weight. Your weighing machine is not functioning well—you must have lost more! It is really strange why women are called the weaker sex—they are not. Man is the weaker sex.

Danny discovered his wife was cheating with another guy, so he went to this guy's wife and told her about it.

"I know what we will do," she said, "let's take revenge on them."

So they went to a motel and had revenge on them.

She said, "Let's have more revenge," and they kept having revenge, revenge. . . .

Finally Danny said, "That's enough revenge—I have no more hard feelings left."

Be a little careful—this is just the beginning!

A couple wakes up after the first night of their honeymoon. She sits up in bed, looks at her husband who is lying naked next to her, and says in a surprised voice, "Darling, did we use him all up in one night?"

Aditya, this happens to almost every new male sannyasin in the beginning: finding so many women here he goes crazy. But within a few weeks he comes to his senses, and then a totally reverse process sets in. First *he* chases women; after a few weeks the women start chasing men and they start escaping.

Many women have reported to me: "What has happened here to male sannyasins? They don't seem to be much interested in women. They don't approach women, they avoid them. Rather than taking the initiative, they escape—the moment they see a woman chasing them, they escape."

What happens in the ordinary world is that man has plenty to imagine, fantasize about, because the society does not allow you many relationships with women—only one woman. And you get tired, you get bored, and your mind starts roaming around. And all the women who don't belong to you look tremendously beautiful, just stunning—because they are not available. Your mind starts fancying, your mind goes into trips.

Here it is totally different. This commune lives in the future now. It is how it is going to be all over the world sooner or later. This commune heralds a new consciousness, a consciousness rooted in freedom. Up to now you have lived in a deep slavery, psychological slavery.

When you *get* freedom, in the beginning you rush into it madly. You start doing all kinds of things that you always wanted to do but you were not permitted to do. Then soon things settle. You become aware that all women are alike just as all men are alike. Maybe there are differences, but they are peripheral. Somebody has black hair and somebody has blonde hair and somebody has blue eyes and somebody has black eyes —just peripheral differences.

But as you become more and more aware of *many* people, as you become related to many people, one thing becomes absolutely clear to you: that *all* men are alike—almost alike—so are all women. Then settling starts. Then you start settling with one woman, with one man, in a more intimate relationship.

That intimacy is not possible in the outside world because your mind will always go on thinking that your woman, your man, has not got that which others have got. And there is no way to find out the truth. Here the way is available; you can find out the truth. And once the truth is known you start settling with one person. And this settlement is not enforced; this is not a legal arrangement. You will not be punished if you separate; nobody is preventing you from separating.

But, still, now you start a totally different kind of journey, a new pilgrimage of intimacy, unimposed intimacy. And now you see that the deeper you want to enter into the other person, the more time is needed, patience is needed, many kinds of situations are needed.

And physical penetration is sex, which is a very superficial thing. Psychological penetration is love, which is far more deep, far more significant, far more beautiful, far more human. The first is animal, the second is human. And then there is a third kind of penetration: when two consciousnesses meet, merge, melt into each other. I call that prayer.

Aditya, move towards prayer, because only prayer will give you *real* contentment. Only prayer will make you aware of the divinity of the other person, of the godliness of the other person. And seeing the godliness of the other person, of your beloved, you will become aware of your own godliness.

Love is a mirror. A real relationship is a mirror in which two lovers see each other's faces and recognize God. It is a path towards God.

The fifth question

Bhagwan,
I am born British and so is my friend!
Any hope?

Vivek,

NOBODY IS BORN BRITISH. It is a disease that happens later on. We learn it; it is not innate. Just like nobody is born German or Indian. These are structures that are imposed on us later on, after the birth. These are social ways of enslaving your psyche, your being. Every society imposes certain forms, rules, regulations. Every society gives you a shape, a form, a face, a facade.

Nobody is British and nobody is German and nobody is Indian. Hence these structures can be dropped, one can slip out of them.

The only thing needed is awareness. We are so unaware that we become one with the structure, identified with it. We start thinking that we *are* it. And that's where the disease becomes a permanent phenomenon; it becomes chronic. Otherwise, one can slip out of being British or Hindu or Mohammedan or communist as easily as the snake gets out of its old skin and never looks back.

Secondly: not all Britishers are British, not all Germans are Germans, not all Indians are Indians. You can find a few Indians here—my sannyasins or my would-be sannyasins; they are not Indians. They have slipped out of the Indian prison. Now, there are so many Germans here, and when I go on telling jokes against Germans they laugh as relaxedly as you laugh. They don't feel hurt.

When I said something against the British, the Britishers were those who were most happy. They were happy because they must be feeling jealous of the Germans! I go on hitting the Germans so much! I have a certain soft corner for Haridas, Govinddas, etcetera—I go on hitting them! And the Britishers must be feeling a little lost, lagging behind!

My sannyasins belong to no race, to no country, to no religion. That's what my sannyas is all about: getting out of all kinds of prisons, becoming simply human; declaring one's universality, declaring that "The whole earth belongs to us."

As sannyasins grow slowly slowly into millions, we are going to create trouble. When I have got enough sannyasins I will tell you, "Now you can burn your passports and move freely from one country to another—because freedom of movement is a birthright."

This is so ugly, that you cannot move from one country to another country easily; they create so many barriers. When you pass the boundary of one country to another you immediately become aware that you have been in a prison and you are entering into another prison. The prison is big, so when you are inside you don't know about it.

The person who has never left India will not be aware that he is living in a big prison, but when you leave the country then you know how difficult it is: how you are tortured for hours, how many papers you have to fill in, how many things you have to do before you can get over the border. Then you know that this is a prison. And you have to do the same thing in the other country. These countries are big prisons.

The hope is that when there are millions of sannyas-ins, and we have created enough orange energy in the world, we will break all these barriers.

But remember always: not all Germans are Germans, not all Britishers are British, not all Indians are Indian. That is the only hope. There are a few who *are* in the prison but not part of it—it is just an accident that they are born in India, an accident that they are born in England; otherwise they are free souls. They are the real hope for humanity, the real hope for the future.

This English sportsman had been abroad and re-turned to his home without notice. While walking through the corridor with his butler, he looked into his bedroom and discovered his wife making love to a strange man.

"Fetch my rifle at once!" he instructed his butler.

In a matter of minutes his rifle was brought to him. Raising it and taking aim, he was tapped on the shoulder by the butler who whispered, "If I may say so, sir, remember you are a true sportsman. Get him on the rise!"

Now the butler is not British, not at all!—has more sense of humor.

Two Englishmen were coming home late at night from a poker party. One said, "I am always afraid when I return home late from a party like this. I shut off the engine of my car a half a block from home and coast in-to the garage. I take off my shoes and sneak into the house. I am as quiet as possible, but invariably, about the time I settle down into bed, my wife sits up and starts to berate me."

The other man said, "You just have the wrong technique. I never have any trouble. I barge into the garage, slam the door, stomp into the house and make a hell of a racket. Then I go upstairs to the bedroom, pat my wife and say, 'How about it, kid?' She always pretends she is asleep.''

The sixth question

Bhagwan,
No passion, no jealousy, and so much loving.
Can it be true that this suffering is over?

Prem Turiya,

THIS IS ONE OF THE MOST FUNDAMENTAL THINGS to be remembered, and you will have to be constantly aware: you cannot take it for granted that the suffering is over. If you take it for granted that the suffering is over, the suffering will be back by the back door. You have to be constantly alert and aware.

Yes, for the moment there is no jealousy, no passion, and yet so much loving—naturally. When there is no passion and no jealousy, all the energies move into the direction of love. It is the same energy that becomes passion, that becomes jealousy. When there is no jealousy, no passion, all the energy is available for the flowers of love to bloom. But don't take it for granted. Don't think that the suffering is over for ever.

Life is a continuous evolution and you have to be constantly alert, otherwise you can fall back into the old patterns very easily. And the old patterns have persisted so long, they have become so ingrained in your blood, in your bones, in your very marrow, that one moment of unconsciousness and you are back. You have to go on being aware.

Something beautiful is happening . . . much more is going to happen. One never knows how much more is possible. We are never aware of our potential unless it becomes actual.

You have seen a beautiful space of non-jealous love. Passion is a kind of fever and it consumes much energy. Fever naturally consumes energy—and passion is fever. When passion disappears, compassion arises. And compassion is cool. Passion is hot, it burns you. Compassion is cool—not cold, remember. Hatred is cold, lust is hot. Exactly between the two is the golden mean, neither hot nor cold. Then you are in a state of cool warmth. Very paradoxical it seems—cool warmth. It is not hot, but it is warm; it is not cold, but it is cool.

And the real flower of love opens up only in that climate of warmth-coolness. A warm coolness is the right climate for the lotus of love to blossom.

But don't take it for granted. Never take anything for granted! Each moment you have to conquer it again and again. Life is a continuous conquest. It is not that once and for all it is settled and then you can fall asleep and stay unconscious and there is no worry left. Again you will be back in the same rut.

Turiya, I am happy—I have been watching you. You *are* looking both warm and cool. It is a non-ending process. Be alert, be watchful. Don't destroy this beautiful flower that is growing in you.

When you have something precious you have to be more aware. When you have nothing to lose you can be unconscious, you can fall asleep; there is no problem. But when you have something to lose—and this is something precious—be more conscious, be more alert. You have discovered a treasure.

The seventh question

Bhagwan,
What is intelligence?

Govindo,

FIRST, KNOW WELL THAT INTELLECTUALITY is not intelligence. To be intellectual is to be phony; it is a pretending intelligence. It is not real because it is not yours; it is borrowed. Intelligence is the growth of inner consciousness. It has nothing to do with knowledge, it has something to do with meditativeness.

An intelligent person does not function out of his past experience; he functions in the present. He does not react, he responds. Hence he is always unpredictable; one can never be certain what he is going to do.

A Catholic, a Protestant and a Jew were talking to a friend who said he had just been given six months to live.

"What would you do," he asked the Catholic, "if your doctor gave you six months to live?"

"Ah!" said the Catholic. "I would give all my belongings to the Church, take communion every Sunday, and say my 'Hail Marys' regularly."

"And you?" he asked the Protestant.

"I would sell up everything and go on a world cruise and have a great time!"

"And you?" he said to the Jew.
"Me? I would see another doctor."

That is intelligence!

Janet, a pert secretary, sashayed into the boss' office. "I have some good news and some bad news," she announced.

"No jokes, please," said her boss. "Not on quarterly report day. Just give me the good news."

"Okay," declared the girl. "The good news is that you are not sterile."

This is intelligence!

The outraged husband discovered his wife in bed with another man. "What is the meaning of this?" he demanded. "Who is this fellow?"

"That seems like a fair question," said the wife, rolling over. "What is your name?"

That is intelligence!

One day the King of Yen visited the Master Chao Chou, who did not even get up when he saw him coming.

The king asked, "Which is higher, a worldly king, or the 'King of Dharma'?"

Chao Chou replied, "Among human kings I am higher; among the Kings of Dharma I am also higher."

Hearing this surprising answer, the king was very pleased.

The next day a general came to visit Chao Chou, who not only got up from his seat when he saw the general coming, but also showed him more hospitality in every way than he had shown to the king.

After the general had left, Chao Chou's attendant monks asked him, "Why did you get up from your seat when a person of lower rank came to see you, yet did not do so for one of the highest rank?"

Chao Chou replied, "You don't understand. When people of the highest quality come to see me, I do not get up from my seat; when they are of middle quality, I do; but when they are of the lowest quality, I go outside of the gate to receive them."

I am Higher

MAN LIVES IN A VERY UPSIDE-DOWN STATE. Hence, whenever there is an enlightened Master, his actions, his words, his behavior, all appear to the ordinary man absurd. Jesus is misunderstood for the simple reason that a man of eyes is talking to the men who are blind. Socrates is not understood for the same reason, because he is talking to people who are utterly deaf. And so has been the case with all the Buddhas of all the countries, of all the races. And, unfortunately, this is going to remain the case forever. It is something in the very nature of things.

Man is unconscious; he understands the language of unconsciousness. And whenever somebody talks from the peaks of consciousness it becomes utterly un-understandable, unintelligible. He is so far away! By the time his words reach the dark valleys of our unconscious we have distorted them to such an extent that they have no reference at all to the origin any more.

The Master looks sometimes mad, sometimes irrational, sometimes stubborn. But the only reason that he cannot behave like you, that he cannot be part of the crowd mind, is that he has become awakened and the crowd is fast asleep.

To understand a Master you have to learn great sympathy; only that will create a bridge. That's what the relationship of a disciple to the Master is. You can listen to a Master without being a disciple. You will hear the words but you will miss the meaning. You will hear the song but you will miss the music. You will hear the argument but you will miss the conclusion. You will know what he is saying but you will not be able to see where he is indicating.

To understand the significance—which is wordless —to understand the meaning, a totally different kind of relationship is needed. It is not that of a speaker and the audience: it is that of two lovers. It has to be a love affair; then only is there sympathy enough to have a bridge, to have communication.

And once the sympathy is there, it is not very far away from empathy. Sympathy can be transformed into empathy very easily; in fact, it changes into empathy of its own accord. Just as you sow seeds and in the right time they sprout and the spring comes and there are many flowers, sow the seeds of sympathy—that is, initiation into disciplehood—then soon there will be flowers of empathy.

In sympathy there is still a little distance. You can hear—you can hear a little better than before, you can understand more clearly than before—but still things are in a state of vagueness: more clear than before but not absolutely clear yet; in a state of twilight. The night is no more but the sun has not risen yet and it is very misty. You can see but can't decipher things accurately.

Empathy means now there is no distance any more. Now the disciple is drowned in the Master—he has become a devotee. Now the Master is drowned in the disciple; they are not separate entities any more. They have reached the same rhythm of being; they pulsate in synchronicity.

Then there is understanding and that understanding liberates, and that understanding is immediate. You see the Master, you look into his eyes, you hear his words, you see him moving, his gestures. . . and they are immediately understood without any translation by the mind. The mind functions no more as a mediator. It is direct communion—not even communication but communion.

The first step is that of a student, curious but still a spectator, far away, collecting information, knowledge. The second step is that of a disciple, no more a spectator but a participant, no more interested in knowledge but tremendously interested in knowing. And the third step is that of a devotee, utterly one with the Master, partaking of his being, drinking out of his inexhaustible source, drunk—drunk with the divine.

Only the devotee understands absolutely, the disciple understands a little bit, the student only hears mere words.

Remember, you have to pass through these stages too. And it all depends on you: one can remain a student forever. If you keep the distance, if you are afraid to come close, you will be here and yet not here.

Come closer—spiritually closer. Bring your beings, unafraid, closer to the Master, closer to his light. Yes, that light is not only light, it is fire too; it is going to consume you. Be consumed, because in that fire there is great hope of a rebirth.

These small Zen stories on the surface look like just ordinary anecdotes—they are not. They carry immense significance. Before we enter into the story, a few things have to be understood.

The other day there was a question from Satsanga. He said, "Bhagwan, why are you not a little more diplomatic with the politicians and the priests?—because that will save us a lot of trouble."

I can understand what he means; I can understand his worry. He would like me to be a little more diplomatic—but a Master cannot be diplomatic. It has never been so, it is impossible. Diplomacy is cunningness, diplomacy is the art of lying. Diplomacy is the way of persuading others without telling them the truth. Diplomacy is a game. Politicians play the game; mystics cannot play it.

A mystic is one who calls a spade a spade. He is straight, whatsoever the cost. He cannot deceive, he cannot lie, he cannot keep quiet. If he sees something he will say it, and he will say it as it is.

Gurdjieff used to say, sometimes to very prominent people, famous in some way or other—great authors, painters, poets, politicians, the people who dominate this world, the great egoists. . . . He used to say to these people a very significant thing—remember it. Suddenly he would say to them, "You have a very good facade."

Now to say to a politician, to a president of a country or to a prime minister or to a king, "You have a very good facade," is to invite trouble. And Gurdjieff lived his whole life in trouble. But there is no other way.

He also used to say, more than once. . . . Whenever some egoist would ask him, "Do you love me? Do you like me?" this was his answer: "For what you could be I have nothing but benevolence, but as you are I hate you—back to your grandmother!"

This is not diplomacy: this is creating enemies.

Jesus must have been a really great artist in creating enemies because he was only thirty-three when he was crucified, and there were only three years of work because he appeared at the age of thirty. Up to that time he was with the mystery schools, going around the world to Egypt, to India, and the possibility is even to Tibet and to Japan.

Hence the Bible has no record of his years of preparation; the record is very abrupt. Something about his childhood is said, very fragmentary. And only once is he mentioned: when he was twelve years of age and he started arguing with the priests in the temple— that's all. Then there is a gap of eighteen years. . . nothing is mentioned.

Now a man like Jesus cannot just live an ordinary life for eighteen years and then suddenly explode into Christhood; that is not possible. These eighteen years he was moving with different Masters, with different systems, getting initiated into different mystery schools, learning whatsoever was available, getting in tune with as many Masters as possible.

He appears at the age of thirty and by the age of thirty-three he is crucified. In three years he really did a good job! He was quick! You cannot think that he was diplomatic; he was the most undiplomatic man ever.

In fact, that's the way the awakened people behave.

What exactly is diplomacy, Satsanga?

"Daddy, what is diplomacy?" asked little Bill, just home from school.

"Well, son, it is like this," replied his dad. "If I were to say to your mother, 'Your face would stop a clock,' that would be stupidity. But if I were to say, 'When I look at you, time stands still,' that is diplomacy!"

Yes, you would like me to be a little more diplomatic; that will save a lot of trouble. But that will save you also from truth, remember. Truth brings many troubles. It is bound to be so because people live in lies, and when you bring truth into the world, their lies, their lives rooted in lies, react. A great antagonism is bound to happen. And people as they are, in their unconsciousness, cannot live without lies.

Friedrich Nietzsche is right. He says, "Please, don't destroy people's lies, their illusions, because if you destroy their illusions they will not be able to live at all; they will collapse." They will not find anything worth living for. They live because of the illusions; the illusions keep on giving them hope. They live in the tomorrow which never comes. They live in their ambitions which are never fulfilled; but whether fulfilled or not, through those ambitions and desires and illusions and expectations and hopes they can drag their lives up to their graves. If you destroy their illusions, they may simply drop dead here and now because then there would be no point in living.

And whenever you think of suicide, remember, why are you thinking of suicide? Some hope has turned sour, some expectation has turned into a frustration, some desire has proved futile. You have become aware; even in your unawareness a little ray of awareness has penetrated you. You have seen, maybe only for a moment, a glimpse, just like lightning in the dark night. For a moment all was light and you have seen that the way you are living is false and there is no fulfillment if you live in a false way. Immediately the idea of suicide arises in you.

More and more people are committing suicide today, more than ever. More people commit suicide in the West than in the East. It looks very strange, very illogical. It should not be so, because in the East people are starving but they don't commit suicide. In the West they have all that man has always desired. People have two houses—one in the city, one in the mountains or on the seabeach, in the country. They have two-car garages. . .and all kinds of gadgets that technology has made available.

For the first time, the West has succeeded in being affluent, but more people are committing suicide there than in the East. Why?—for the simple reason that the East can still hope and the West is becoming aware that there is no hope. When you don't have something you can hope for it; when you have it, how can you hope any more? The thing is there and nothing has happened through it. You have the money, you have a good wife, children, husband, prestige, respectability —and suddenly you become aware in this affluence that deep down you are hollow, poor, a beggar and nothing else. The whole effort of achieving all these things has failed. Things are there, but no fulfillment has happened through them. This is the cause of more suicide in the West.

In the West, too, more Americans commit suicide than anybody else because they are the most affluent, they are the most in a state of shock: ''All the hopes for which we have lived for centuries are fulfilled, and yet nothing is fulfilled." And this is going to be so more and more: more and more people will commit suicide.

Friedrich Nietzsche is correct: the ordinary man cannot live without illusions. Don't take his illusions away from him!

And the Master does exactly that: he tries to take your illusions away. He creates a situation in which, ordinarily, you would commit suicide. But if you are fortunate enough to have a communion with a Master, the same situation creates sannyas. It is the same situation, the *same* crisis!

This is my observation: that true sannyas happens only when you have come to the verge of suicide. When you see that the outside world is finished, then there are only two alternatives left: either commit suicide and be finished because there is nothing to live for any more, or turn in. "The outer world has failed, now let us try the inner": that is sannyas. Sannyas and suicide are two aspects of the same coin. If you are focussed and obsessed with the outside, then suicide; if you are a little loose, flexible, then sannyas.

But a Master cannot be diplomatic. He has to create this crisis in which suicide *is* possible—and also sannyas, also transformation, also a new birth. But a new birth is possible only when you die to the old, when you die to the past.

Cynthia's fine figure had been poured into a beautiful form-fitting gown and she made a point of calling her date's attention to it over and over again throughout the evening.

Finally, over a nightcap in his apartment, he said, "You have been talking about that dress all evening long. You called my attention to it first when we met for cocktails, mentioned it again at dinner, and still again at the theater. Now that we are here alone in my penthouse, what do you say if we drop the subject?''

This is diplomacy! But Masters simply call a spade a spade. Their truth is utterly nude; whether you like it or not is not the point. They cannot compromise with your likings. If they start compromising with your likings thay can't be of any help to you. To compromise with you means to compromise with your sleep, your unconsciousness, your mechanicalness. To compromise with you means to stop waking you up. That is not possible.

Hence, Satsanga, I cannot be diplomatic. Moreover, I am not British.

Just the other day I was talking about poor Anurag's mother—a perfect British lady!—but she was not here, just as expected. She had been here only once in many weeks. She simply goes on sitting in the hotel, utterly bored—as every British person is bored! Poor Anurag —I call her ''poor'' because she is going through something really horrible. Now I have to call it horrible, I can't be diplomatic! She arranged so that her mother could listen to the tape, and after she listened to the tape Anurag asked her, ''What do you think of it?'' She said, ''Dear, I fell asleep.''

This is diplomacy!

People listen only to that which they want to listen to; otherwise they fall asleep. At least they can think of a thousand other things, and that too is a kind of sleep because they are no longer listening.

I have to be hard! I have to be as hard as possible because your sleep is deep and it has to be shattered. I have to hit your head with a hammer, otherwise you are not going to wake up. For centuries you have been asleep; sleep has become your nature. You have forgotten what awareness is, what to be awake means.

THERE ARE THREE TYPES OF MEN, and the Master behaves differently according to the type. The highest type is the man who has tasted the joy of no-mind. The Master behaves with that type of man in a totally different way, because he knows he will understand.

The state of no-mind is the highest state. You are at the peak when you are in the state of no-mind, when you are absolutely silent, when nothing stirs within you, no idea, no thought, when the mind has ceased to create noise, the constant noise. The mind is chattering so much that it won't allow you to hear anything. When the mind's chattering ceases, for the first time you become aware of the music of your own being. And for the first time you also become aware of the music that this existence is.

When such a man approaches a Master, the Master behaves in a totally different way—because he knows whatsoever he does he will be understood. Communion is possible because there is no barrier.

The second type of man is the man who lives in between, between the first and the third. He has a meditative mind—not a no-mind yet, but a meditative mind. That is, he is on the way. He has learned how to be a little silent, a little more harmonious than others. The noise is there, but it is a distant noise; he has been able to detach himself from it. He has created a little distance between himself and his mind; he is no more identified with the mind. He does not think, "I am the mind." The mind is there, still chattering, still playing old tricks, but the man is a little alert not to be a slave of the mind. The mind has not left him, but the mind is no longer so powerful as it ordinarily is.

In the state of no-mind, the mind has left; the mind has become tired. The mind has come to realize that "This man has gone beyond—beyond my powers. Now this man cannot be exploited any more. This man has become utterly unidentified with me. He will use me but I cannot use him."

The second type of man, who is in between, sometimes falls back into the old pattern, is *used* by the mind, sometimes gets out of the old pattern. It is hide-and-seek. Mind is still not absolutely certain that it has failed; there is still hope, because once in a while the man starts listening to the mind, becomes again identified. The distance is not great; the mind is very close. Any moment—any moment of unconsciousness—and the mind takes over, starts bossing over him again.

This is the second type of man: the meditative man, who has known a few glimpses of the eternal. Just as you can see the Himalayas from thousands of miles away . . . the snow-covered peaks in the early morning sun in an open sky, unclouded sky, can be seen from thousands of miles away. That is one thing; and to be on the peak, to abide there, is quite another.

The first type of man *abides* in no-mind. The second type of man has glimpses only—of tremendous value of course, because those glimpses will pave the way so that he can reach the peak. Once you have seen the peak, even from thousands of miles away, the invitation has been received. Now you cannot remain in the world at rest, in the old way. Something starts challenging you, something starts calling you forth. An adventure has taken possession of you: you *have* to travel to the peak. It may take years, maybe lives, but the journey has started. The first seed has fallen into the heart.

The Master behaves with the meditative man in a different way, because with the first, communion is possible, with the second, communication is possible.

And then there is the third type: the man who lives identified with the mind, with the ego, with whom even communication is not possible, with whom there is no way to relate.

This word "identification" is beautiful. It means to make something an entity, to entity-fy the "id"; that is the meaning of identification. When *you* become the mind you have become a thing; you are no more separate. You have fallen in sleep. This is what is called metaphysical sleep. You have lost track of your own self. You have forgotten your reality and you have become one with something which you are not. To become one with something that you are not is identification; and to be that which you are is dis-identification.

The first man lives in dis-identification. He knows he is not the body, he is not the mind. He simply knows he is only awareness and nothing else. The body goes on changing, the mind goes on changing, but there is one thing in you which is unchanging, absolutely unchanging; that is your awareness. It was exactly the same when you were a child and it will remain exactly the same when you are an old man. It was the same when you were born and it will be the same when you die. It was the same before your birth, it will be the same after your death. It is the *only* thing in existence which is eternal, unchanging, the only thing that abides.

And only this eternal awareness can be the true home, nothing else, because everything else is a flux. And we go on clinging to the changing; then we create misery, because it changes and we want it not to change. We are asking for the impossible, and because the impossible cannot happen we fall into misery again and again.

The young man wants to remain young forever; that is not possible. He will have to become old, the body will have to become old. And when the body is old he will be miserable. But awareness is the same. The body is just like the house; awareness is the host. Deep down within your body and mind complex there is a totally different phenomenon constantly happening. It is neither body nor mind; it is something that can observe body and mind both. It is pure observation. It is the witnessing soul—*sakshin*. The first type of man knows that he is unidentified with all that is changing. He is centered in his reality. The third type of man is obsessed with something which he is not. In fact, the majority of people belong to the third type. The third type is metaphysically ill. If you ask the awakened one, then the third type is mad, insane. To think yourself something which you are not is insanity.

A man went to a psychiatrist and said, "Doctor, you will have to help me. I can't help thinking that I am a dog. I even chew bones, bark, and lie on the mat in the evenings."

Said the psychiatrist, "Just lie on that couch. . . ."

"I am not allowed to!" he cried.

But this is the situation of the ordinary humanity. Somebody has become a Hindu, somebody has become a Mohammedan, somebody has become a Christian. Somebody is Indian, somebody is Chinese, somebody is Italian. These are all identifications. Somebody thinks himself white, somebody thinks himself black. Somebody thinks himself a man and somebody is identified with being a woman. These are all states of deep unconscious slumber.

If you are not the body, how can you be a man or a woman? If you are not the body, how can you be white or black? If you are not even the mind, how can you be Christian or Hindu? If you are only awareness, then you are only awareness and nothing else.

Now this little Zen story:

One day the King of Yen visited the Master Chao Chou, who did not even get up when he saw him coming.

THAT IS STRANGE! First: now it has become almost impossible for a president or a prime minister or a king to go to a Master, because they think they are powerful people. Why should they go to these poor people? What can they give to them? Values have changed.

Within these two thousand years, man's values have gone through immense change. In the ancient days, the highest man was not the one who had power but the one who had renounced power. And it seems significant that the one who has renounced power should be thought higher; it is a very ordinary desire to be powerful. The man who has been able to renounce power has attained to a certain inner integrity. He has dropped a very ordinary ambition; he has become extraordinary.

In those days, kings used to go to seek advice, to search for light, to sit at the feet of somebody who had attained.

This king must have heard of Chao Chou. He went to see him. This shows a totally different priority. It is very difficult now; it is difficult because man has become more materialistic. His mind is too much concerned with what you have rather than with what you are. In the ancient days the value was not in your possessions but in your being. The value was not in your things, not even in your knowledge—because that too is a possession—but in your being, in your sheer being, in the purity of your inner core. You may have nothing. . . .

Alexander had gone to see Diogenes—a naked man who had nothing. But it is beautiful to remember that even Alexander the Great had the guts to go to Diogenes, the naked *fakir*. For what had he gone? Alexander's generals, his prime minister, his ministers, were all against it. They said, "For what are you going there? That man has nothing!"

Alexander said, "I know it, that that man has nothing; that's why I am going to see him, because I have heard he has a tremendous rootedness, a great centeredness—and I want to see a centered man. I am just fragmentary, I have no center. I don't know what it is to have a center and I want to see a person who has a center. He possesses nothing on the outside, but he possesses himself—and that is the real possession."

One day the King of Yen visited the Master Chao Chou, who did not even get up when he saw him coming.

And Chao Chou did not get up. That would have been normal, expected. When the king comes to see you, you have to get up and receive him; it is just a formality.

I have heard that Chuang Tzu, a Taoist Master, used to be in the service of the King of China. Then he left the service. After a few years the king came to hear that Chuang Tzu had become enlightened, so he went to see him.

Chuang Tzu was a man of great manners, formality, because he had been one of the most important men in the court of the king. So the king was expecting the same court manners. When he reached Chuang Tzu, he was playing on his flute, both his legs spread underneath a tree, leaning against the tree. He continued to play on the flute with legs spread.

The king stood there, could not believe his eyes. He said, "Have you gone mad or something? Have you forgotten all court manners?"

Chuang Tzu laughed and he said, "I was showing those manners because I was still hankering for respectability. Now I don't hanker for anything, so why should I care? You may be the king, you may be the beggar—it is all the same to me. Because now I have no desires any more, it does not matter whether the king comes to me or the beggar."

The king was immensely impressed; he understood the point. All those court manners were nothing but ways of buttressing the king.

You buttress somebody, and then in response he buttresses your ego. It is a mutual kind of arrangement. You say good things about others and they say good things about you. Both are being formal because both want to hear good things about themselves.

Chuang Tzu said, "Now it is up to you, whatsoever you think. You can think I have gone mad, you can think I have fallen from grace. Who cares?"

Exactly the same happened with Chao Chou: he did not even get up when he saw the king coming. But this king must have had a totally different quality from the king who visited Chuang Tzu. Even Alexander was offended by Diogenes' behavior, because Diogenes was lying down naked on the bank of a river in the sand. It was early morning—must have been a morning like this, very cool—and he was taking a sunbath. He didn't get up; he remained lying down, taking a sunbath.

Alexander was a little embarrassed—how to start talking with this man? Not finding anything else, he said, "I have come to see you—I am Alexander the Great. Can I be of any help to you?"

Diogenes said, "Look, if you are really great, you need not go on declaring it. That simply shows a very stupid mind. That shows only a very small mind, egoistic. To declare yourself great simply means you are suffering from an inferiority complex!

"And the second thing: I don't need anything, but if you really want to help me you can do one thing—just stand aside, because you are blocking the sun."

That was all that Diogenes asked from Alexander the Great: "Stand aside, don't come in the way of the sun and me."

But Alexander could not understand Diogenes. Of course he was impressed, but in a totally different manner. He was impressed by the powerful presence of Diogenes—it was as if the whole bank was full of his presence, as if he was creating a Buddhafield. Although he was armored, although he was not at all interested in mysticism, he was impressed.

But this King of Yen must have been of the first type, far higher than the king who visited Chuang Tzu and far higher than Alexander. He understood it.

> *The king asked, "Which is higher, a worldly*
> *king, or the 'King of Dharma'?"*

Why did he ask this question? You will be surprised to know that he asked it just to see whether Chao Chou showed any so-called humility or not.

The religious people always go on showing humbleness: "I am nothing, I am nobody." And if you look into their eyes, their eyes are saying just the opposite. If you watch their behavior, it is always a projection of holier-than-thou. They go on saying, "We are nothing," and they go on in a subtle way, in a diplomatic way, proclaiming, "We are saints."

> *The king asked, "Which is higher, a*
> *worldly king, or the 'King of Dharma'?"*
>
> *Chao Chou replied, "Among human kings*
> *I am higher; among the Kings of Dharma I*
> *am also higher."*

T HE REAL MAN OF ZEN IS NOT HUMBLE in the ordinary sense of the word. He simply says whatsoever is the case. This is the case! Chao Chou is simply stating a truth. He is not saying anything about himself, remember. He is simply stating a fact: *"This* state—this state of no-mind in which I am—is higher, higher among human kings and higher among Kings of Dharma also—because it is the highest state."

Once Ramakrishna was given a painting by a great painter—a painting of Ramakrishna himself, a portrait. Ramakrishna took the painting, bowed down to the painting, touched the feet—his own feet, it was his own portrait! The painter was puzzled: "Is that man really mad?" The disciples were puzzled.

One disciple asked, "Paramahansadeva, what are you doing, touching your own feet?"

Ramakrishna said, "Right! You should have reminded me before. I should not do such a thing. What will people think? They will think I am mad! But the truth is, I completely forgot that this is my picture—I could only see the ultimate state of consciousness. This is a portrait of *samadhi,* not of Ramakrishna. Ramakrishna is irrelevant! It could have been Buddha's picture, it could have been Krishna's picture, it could have been Jesus' picture. It is just an accident that it is mine. It doesn't matter.

"But the painter has been able to catch hold of something very subtle; he has been able to depict something which is indescribable. And I could not resist myself—I had to bow down, I had to touch the feet."

Remember, when Chao Chou says:

"Among human kings I am higher; among the Kings of Dharma, I am also higher . . ."

he is not talking about himself, not at all. He is talking about the ultimate state. He is no more, so who is there to be humble? See the point: there is nobody to be proud, there is nobody to be humble. Those are all games of the ego—to be humble or to be proud.

The real man is neither proud nor humble; he simply is not. Then whatsoever he says has no reference to his personality. He is only a mirror; he reflects the ultimate.

Chao Chou is talking about the ultimate. He has become one with the ultimate. And the king understood it.

Hearing this surprising answer. . . .

The answer is really surprising. When you go to saints, they don't talk like that.

Once I was invited to a religious conference. Three hundred saints were invited from all over the country. I was puzzled why they invited me, because I am not a saint. It seems by some mistake. . . .

They had made a great platform for all three hundred saints to sit together, but they were not ready to sit on the same platform, at the same height, with others. *Nobody* was ready! They all wanted a little higher place than the others. Now, that was impossible! How can you manage three hundred people, everybody asking for a little higher place than the other? So the stage was for three hundred people, and thousands of people had gathered to listen, but each saint talked to the people— sitting alone on that big platform.

It was impossible to even bring them together. And if you talk to them they will all say, "We are just dust and nothing else. We are humble people, servants of God, servants of humanity."

Even once a year some of them would wash the feet of a poor man—all formality! But they could not sit on the same platform. One of those three hundred saints had brought his own golden throne and he wanted to sit on his golden throne. Now the others were very angry. They said, "This cannot be allowed! If he sits on a golden throne, then we also need golden thrones of the same height."

Can you see what kind of people these are? Are these

saints or monkeys? Even monkeys are not so stupid! I
have seen them just sitting in trees, on the same
branches, enjoying themselves. Nobody is worried
about who is higher, who is lower.

But if you talk to these saints . . . and they all ad-
dressed the audience, and with great humbleness.
Pious egoism! Religious egoism! And the pious,
religious egoism is far more dangerous than any other.
All their behavior, all their talk, is only a beautiful
facade, a cultivated phenomenon. Because people
respect humbleness they are pretending to be
humble—in order to be respected. You see the strategy
and the cunning ways of the ego? And these are the
people who have reduced the whole of religion to formality.

Hearing this surprising answer . . .

It was really surprising—surprising because ordinarily
the religious people don't talk like that. The king must
have expected that he would say, "I am nobody. I am
just dust under your feet. I am the servant of humanity,
just a servant of God. I am here to serve others."

But he simply said, "No. I am higher than the human
kings and I am higher than the Kings of Dharma too."
He simply stated the fact. In fact, he is showing great
respect to the king. By saying the truth he is saying, "I
understand that you can understand."

*Hearing this surprising answer, the king was
very pleased.*

Reading this sentence for the first time, you will be a little surprised why the king is pleased. He should really
be displeased because this man is trying to prove himself higher than everybody—not only than him but

than other saints also. He is saying, "I am greater than the Kings of Dharma."

But he was pleased. Why?—for the simple reason that this man understands that the king can understand—and more respect than that cannot be shown. He has said the truth as it is, naked, utterly naked, trusting that here is a man who will be able to understand. There is no need to compromise; there is no need to come down; there is no need to talk in a language that *he* can understand. You can say the truth as it is and still you can hope that he will understand.

Chao Chou must have seen that this man had attained something of the no-mind.

And whenever you come before a Master, just a look is enough and he knows you through and through, to the innermost core. He becomes immediately acquainted with you; no other introduction is needed. He can see whether you are asleep or awake. He can see whether you are pretending or real. He can see whether you are pseudo or authentic. He can see where you are.

Every evening people come to see me; they come to touch my feet. Touching my feet has nothing to do with me; that is just an excuse for them to bow down, to surrender. Any other excuse will do. If you can manage you can bow down to a tree, and immediately you will see a great uprising in yourself, a great uplift.

There are a few fools also. They will touch my feet, but they are only following a formality. There are a few other kinds of fools who will come to touch my feet but will not even be able to do it formally. They will just sit there like rocks. I touch their heads not to offend them, otherwise it is not worth it because it is meaningless. If they are not surrendering, my touch cannot reach their hearts, my energy cannot stir their hearts. If they are sitting like rocks, they are just touching my feet in a pseudo way. Touching their heads is futile. Still I touch, just not to hurt them unnecessarily. And they will not understand even that. You can hit only when somebody understands.

Now Chao Chou has hit the king as hard as possible by saying, "What are you? I am higher than all the kings, of this world and the other world." He has hit him hard—must have see the immense capacity of the man to understand. And that's why the king is very pleased: he was not hoping that he would be respected so much.

Do you see the point? It is not an ordinary anecdote. When you read it, it looks ordinary; when you go deep into it meditatively, you will find subtle nuances, subtle turns. Just this single phrase—*the king was very pleased*—is of immense importance. What is there to be pleased about? The man has hit him like anything! But there is something to be pleased about, because he thought him worthy enough to hit; he thought him worthy enough to say the truth as it is. He belongs to the first category.

The next day a general came to visit Chao Chou, who not only got up from his seat when he saw the general coming, but also showed him more hospitality in every way than he had shown to the king.

After the general had left, Chao Chou's attendant monks asked him, "Why did you get up from your seat when a person of lower rank came to see you, yet did not do so for one of the highest rank?"

NOW THE ATTENDANT MONKS can see only the outer shell. The general is of a lower rank, the king is of a higher rank—they can only see the outer side. And they must have been puzzled: "Why did Chao Chou behave in such a hard way with the king and why did he behave in such a soft way with the general?"

Chao Chou replied, "You don't understand.
When people of the highest quality come to see
me, I do not get up from my seat . . ."

There is no need, because the highest quality people have no egos; that's why they are of the highest quality. If they have no egos, there is no need to stand up or to show great respect to them. That will be futile, meaningless. That will simply show that you don't understand.

"When people of the highest quality
come to see me, I do not get up from my seat;
when they are of middle quality, I do; but when
they are of the lowest quality, I go outside of
the gate to receive them."

THE WAYS OF THE MASTERS ARE STRANGE! And to be with a Master is to be with a mystery. A Master *is* a mystery: he lives on the earth and yet he is not part of the earth. He is in the body and he is not the body. He uses the mind and he is not the mind. He is in time but he belongs to the beyond, to eternity. He is as alive as you are, but in a totally different way because he knows there is no birth, no death. He has gone beyond life and death; he knows life eternal.

From the outside he is just like you—hungry he eats, thirsty he drinks, tired he sleeps—just like you. But in his innermost core he is totally different because he is in a totally different world, in a totally different space.

And to understand his inner world you will have to grow into your own interiority; that is the only way. You can understand only so much. If you move deep into yourself you will understand the Master in a deep way. The deeper you move inside, the deeper you will understand the Master. To understand the Master you will have to go deeper into yourself. When you have reached the innermost core of your being you will know the Master in his absolute perfection. Otherwise, you will misunderstand.

Now, even the attendant monks could not understand.

> *Chao Chou said, "You don't understand."*

It is *very* simple!

> *"When the people of the highest quality come to see me, I do not get up from my seat . . ."*

"In that way I show my respect to them. I say to them, 'I have seen that you have known something of the no-mind, that your ego is no more a solid phenomenon, it is no more substantial; that you don't hanker for respect. That's why I am not showing you the formal respect. I know that you have gone beyond the form and beyond the formal.' "

We live in the form and in the formal; we change everything into a formality. Love becomes marriage. Christ becomes the church. Buddha is reduced to stone statues. Great truths become ordinary scriptures to be worshipped. We are really very skillful in reducing every higher thing to the lowest possible. We bring everything to our level.

Rather than going to the level of the Buddhas, of the Masters, we bring the Masters, once they have left the world. . . . Of course, when they are alive you cannot bring them to your level; they live without any compromise. You have to surrender to them. But once they are gone, then it is very easy: you can make their statues and temples and you can worship them, and everything becomes formal—Sunday religion—comfortable, convenient, but meaningless.

One Hell's Angel remarked to another, "I don't see you at the gang bangs any more. What happened?"

"I got married," said his buddy.

"No shit, man," said the first cycler, "is legal tail any better than the normal kind?"

"It ain't even so good," said the new groom, "but you don't have to stand in line for it."

It is comfortable, it is convenient—the legal tail! And man is more interested in convenience than in truth, more interested in comfort than in truth, more interested in security than in transformation.

If that is your state too you are going to miss me, because my interest is not security; I will force you more and more into insecurity. My interest is not convenience; I will force you more and more into rebellion. My interest is only one: truth, because it is truth that liberates; everything else becomes a bondage.

THE HIGHEST QUALITY MAN immediately becomes a devotee. The middle quality man immediately becomes a disciple. The lowest quality man remains for years, for lives, just a student.

Look into yourself, where you are. Don't be just a student here. This is not a school; in fact, the whole process is one of de-schooling. I am not teaching you anything; I am here to help you be transformed. I am not giving you a dogma or a creed or a religion; I am not interested in all these things. I simply want to give you that which you already have—it has only to be provoked.

You have to become attuned to me, in deep accord, one with me. Only then will you be benefited. Great benediction can be yours, great blessings can be yours, but you will have to come out of your small prisons, out of your small minds, out of your small egos. And you will get only that which you deserve, which you are worthy of. I can go on showering diamonds on you, but if you don't understand what a diamond is you will go on collecting colored stones.

And people are really so asleep that they don't know what they are doing and they ask for wrong things. They ask for respect, they ask for some nourishment for their egos.

Many people write letters to me—newcomers—saying, "Why in your ashram isn't a little more love shown to us newcomers? Why does everybody seem to be a little aloof, a little cool? Why don't people seem to be interested in newcomers? We come here to find love, warmth."

In fact, behind these words—"love," "warmth," etcetera—all that they are hankering for is some kind of respect, some kind of ego nourishment. That's why people will look cool, people will look aloof.

We are not interested in helping your egos because we don't want to create greater hells for you. You are already in suffering—you have suffered enough. We want to pull you out of your egos. Just a small thing can hurt, just a very small thing. And we have managed things in such a way that there are many things which are bound to hurt your egos. Unless you are ready to drop them you will escape from this place sooner or later.

Only those who are ready to drop their egos will become part of this commune. And this commune is happening after many centuries. There have been Masters with a few disciples. . . . My effort is to bring such a revolution that the whole consciousness of humanity is affected by it. Just individual enlightenment is not enough. We have to start a process of enlightenment in which thousands of people become enlightened almost simultaneously, so that the whole consciousness of humanity can be raised to a higher level because that is the only hope of saving it.

Otherwise, these twenty years are going to be fatal. Either we will succeed in transforming the consciousness of the whole of humanity and bring it to a higher level—at least to the second level, a meditative mind, for millions of people, and for thousands of people to the first grade, the no-mind. . . . If we can do it, that is the only possible way to save humanity. Otherwise, in the hands of foolish politicians so much power has come that *any* moment the third world war can start, and that will destroy the whole of humanity. And all the work of the ages, of all the Buddhas, will be simply destroyed.

Krishna, Jesus, Lao Tzu, Buddha, Pythagoras, Socrates: these people have worked hard to create this garden. And now we are getting ready to burn it totally.

Before it is too late . . . wake up! At least move to the second state of mind—meditative mind—then the first will become easy. Being with me don't be of the third, because that is not really being with me. Only the second is a little bit with me and is on the way to being totally with me. But remember, the goal is to be of the first: no-mind is the goal.

From mind to no-mind is the revolution of sannyas.

Dying Into the Master

The first question

Bhagwan,
I have heard that John the Baptist nearly
drowned his disciples when baptizing them.
Is this true? Is this type of experience something
through which a disciple must pass?

Anand Navin,

IT IS TRUE. I KNOW THIS FELLOW John the Baptist! In fact, every Master has been doing that. It is absolutely necessary because the disciple has to pass through a death process. Unless he dies—dies to his past, dies to his knowledge, dies to his beliefs—he cannot be reborn. And baptism is only symbolic: it is the symbol of death and resurrection.

That's exactly what *I* am doing here. You cling to your beliefs—political, social, religious, philosophical. You cling to whatsoever you have accumulated—although it is all junk, although it has not given you a single glimpse of truth, you cling to it.

Somebody has asked: "I was initiated by a Master five years ago, and now I am feeling deeply interested in you. But the problem is: can a man have two Masters?"

If your first initiation has opened the door to truth, there is no need for me to work on you. Why waste my time? I have so many other people to work upon. If the first Master has not been able to open the door, or you have not allowed him to open the door, or who knows whether he was a Master or not, then why not drop him?

One cannot have two Masters; that is utterly stupid. If the first has done the work then I am not needed; if the first has not done the work, for whatever reason—he may be a pseudo Master, you may have been a pseudo disciple. . . . Something must have gone wrong somewhere. One thing is certain: that that initiation did not work. He could not drown you, he could not kill you—you are still there. But you don't want to drop your old Master and whatsoever he has taught you.

Now you are asking me: "Can a man have two Masters?" I don't accept such people because this is the wrong type of people. Sooner or later you will go to a third person and you will ask: "Can a man have three Masters?"

The first thing to remember here is: to be with me means you disconnect yourself from your past, whatsoever it is—your initiation, your Master, your church, your religion. Unless you disconnect yourself you can't be with me. To be with me you have to be reborn; you have to be a new being, utterly fresh as the dewdrops in the early sun. Less than that won't do. You have to pass through fire. And it is very difficult to pass through fire, because one can see that the familiar is disappearing and the promised is far away. The promised land may be, may not be, and the familiar is going out of your hands. And the mind says, "It is better to have half the bread that you already have than to lose it for the whole bread which you don't have, which is only a promise."

A Master is only a promise: a promise of something that can happen, a promise of your potential becoming actual, a promise of a flowering. But right now you are only a seed, and the seed cannot believe in the promise; it is very difficult for the seed to believe in the promise. The seed would like to remain a seed and yet be a flower. So we go on clinging to the familiar beliefs, systems of thought, ideology. And still we want to be reborn!

It is like a child who wants to cling to the womb and yet wants to be born. That is impossible. Either he has to be in the womb and die in the womb—because after nine months to be in the womb is going to be sure death—or he has to take the risk, the adventure, of going into the unknown.

And, certainly, the child must feel the birth as death. It is death to his life as he has known it up to now: for nine months the darkness, the soothing darkness of the womb, the warmth, the absolutely responsibility-free existence, total rest, relaxation. And he has been floating, swimming, in a body-temperature liquid. He has never lacked anything; all was supplied by the body of the mother. Even before he needed anything it was there, ready to be given to him. Now suddenly he is being thrown out of his home into the unknown. Who knows what is going to happen? He is being uprooted. He clings! It is natural to cling.

And that's exactly the situation when you are with a Master: you have lived in a psychological womb. When you are with a Master he starts pulling you out of your psychological womb. It is far more difficult than the physical process of leaving the womb because you feel closer to the psychological womb. You are a Christian, you are a Hindu, a Mohammedan, and you would like to remain that. And still you want to be transformed. Then you are in a double bind, then you are split.

Two Masters can only mean a deep split in you. I am not here to create schizophrenia. No, one cannot have two Masters—one is more than enough!

You have heard rightly, Navin: . . . *John the Baptist nearly drowned his disciples when baptizing them.*

That's the only way to baptize.

You ask me: *Is this type of experience something through which a disciple must pass?*

Yes, it is a must. Unless the disciple passes through it he never becomes a devotee. And unless you become a devotee you don't know what it means to be with a Master. It is not an intellectual relationship; it is a deep merger with the being of the Master. It is something very existential.

The second question

Bhagwan,
I thought you knew everything. I thought that's what being enlightened is about: knowing. But

you don't know about women, and that they
trust precisely because they know each other's
heart. Women's hate for women is a male myth
invented to keep women separate and power-
less. Who wants to be a man?
Bhagwan, I am totally upset. How can you talk
nonsense? My mind is having a fit and so is my
heart. What to do?

Prem Judy,

YOU MUST BE CARRYING TOO MUCH OF THE CRAP that the Women's Liberation Movement is creating. You are too full of it. Next time you come to me I will have to look into your eyes, because when people are too full of crap, up to their heads, their eyes are brown! And you must have some lesbian tendencies.

You say: *I thought you knew everything.*

You are absolutely wrong—I know nothing. *Not knowing is the most intimate.*

If you have come here with this idea, you have come to a wrong person and to a wrong place. We celebrate ignorance! We destroy all kinds of knowledge. Our whole effort is to bring innocence back to you, the innocence that you had before you were born. The Zen people call it the original face. The innocence is intrinsic. Knowledge is given to you by the society, by the people around you, by the family. Innocence is yours: knowledge is always of others. The more knowledgeable you are, the less you are yourself.

Enlightenment has nothing to do with knowledge. It is freedom from knowledge, it is absolute transcendence of knowledge. It is going beyond knowing.

That's why we started this series of talks with the great sutra: *Not knowing is the most intimate.*

An enlightened person is one who has no barrier between him and existence. And knowledge *is* a barrier. Knowledge divides you from existence; it keeps you separate. Not knowing unites you. Love is a way of innocence. Innocence is a bridge: knowledge is a wall. Who has ever heard of knowledgeable people becoming enlightened? They are the farthest away from enlightenment. Enlightenment grows only in the soil of innocence.

Innocence means childlike wonder, awe. The enlightened person is one who is continuously wondering—because he knows nothing, so everything becomes again a mystery. When you know, things are demystified; when you don't know, they are *re*-mystified. The more you know, the less wonder is in your heart. The more you know, the less you feel the great experience of awe. You cannot say *"Ah, this!"* You cannot be ecstatic. The knowledgeable person is so burdened that he cannot dance, he cannot sing, he cannot love. For the knowledgeable there is no God, because God only means wonder, awe, mystery. That's why, as knowledge has grown in the world, God has become further and further away.

Friedrich Nietzsche could declare that God is dead because of his knowledgeability. He was certainly a great philosopher, and philosophy is bound to come to the conclusion that there is no God because God simply means the mysterious, the miraculous. And knowledge reduces every miracle to ordinary laws; every mystery is reduced to formulas.

Ask the knowledgeable person "What is love?" and he will say, "Nothing but chemistry, the attraction be-

tween male and female hormones. It is no more important than a magnet attracting iron pieces; it is the same
—like negative and positive electricity. Man and
woman are bio-electricity.''

Then everything is destroyed. Then all love and all
poetry and all music are reduced to nonsense. The
lotus is reduced to the mud. The lotus certainly grows
out of the mud, but the lotus is not the mud. It is not
the sum total of its parts; it is more than the sum total of
the parts. That *more* is God, that *more* is poetry, that
more is love. But science has no place for the ''more.''
Science reduces every phenomenon to a mechanical
thing. And do you know what ''science'' means? ''Science'' means knowledge; the actual word ''science''
means knowledge.

Religion is not knowledge; it is just the opposite of
knowledge. It is poetry, it is love. It is basically absurd.
Yes, you can say that I am talking nonsense. If science
is sense then religion *is* nonsense. But that's the beauty
of it.

You say, Judy: *I thought you knew everything.*

That is *your* thought—and I am not here to oblige everybody's thought. I cannot be according to *your*
thoughts. I have more than one hundred thousand
sannyasins; if I am to fulfil everybody's thought I will
be absolutely torn apart, into millions of pieces. I cannot fulfil your ideas about me; that is *your* mistake. And
it is not too late—either drop that idea if you want to be
here with me. . . .

You *are* here with a paradoxical person, with a person who is trying to convey something mysterious to
you—not knowledge—who is trying to pour his experience of wonder and awe into your beings—it is more

like wine than like knowledge—who is trying to make
you intoxicated, who is trying to transform you into
drunkards. Yes, for the rational person it will look like
nonsense.

That's what one of the most important thinkers of
the West, Arthur Koestler, has written about Zen. He
calls it "all nonsense." If you look rationally, it is—but
is reason the only way to approach reality? There are
other ways, far deeper, far more intimate—*not knowing is the most intimate.*

I am not a man of knowledge, although I use words.
I am not even a man of words.

"I am a man of few words. Will you or won't you?"
"Your apartment or mine?" said the chick.
"Look," he said, "if there's going to be such a lot of
discussion about it, let's forget the whole damn thing!"

I use words, but I am not a man of words. It is just
out of sheer necessity: it is because of you that I have to
use words, because you won't understand the wordless. I am waiting eagerly for the day when I will be
able to drop words. I am utterly tired . . . because
words can't convey that which I am and I have to go
on trying to do something which is not possible.

Get ready soon so that we can sit in silence and listen
to the birds or to the wind in the trees. Just *sitting
silently doing nothing, the spring comes and the grass
grows by itself.* That is going to be my ultimate message
and my final work on the earth.

You say: *I thought that's what being enlightened is about: knowing.*

You cannot think anything about enlightenment, and
whatsoever you think is bound to be wrong. It has

nothing to do with knowing; it is a state of not knowing.

But you don't know about women and that
they trust precisely because they know each
other's heart.

I know about nothing. What to say about women?—I don't even know about men! So don't be worried about that. If you know what a woman is or what a man is, beware of your knowledge, because that is not real knowing; it is just opinion that you have gathered.

Yes, man has been propagating ideas against women; now women are propagating ideas against men. It is the *same* foolish thing! And we go on doing this: we go on moving from one extreme to another extreme.

Now, you say: *Women's hate for women is a*
male myth invented to keep women separate
and powerless.

Man has created many myths about women, but now the women are doing the same. They are creating myths about men which are as false as man's myths about women. But I am not here to decide which myth is right and which myth is wrong. I am not here to make you a propagandist for women or against women. My work consists in freeing you from man/woman duality.

And now you say: *Who wants to be a man?*

Judy, if you really don't want to be a man you would not have written this. It is just like the ancient parable of the fox who was trying to reach the grapes and could not reach: the grapes were too high. She tried and tried, and failed again and again. Then she looked around—foxes are very cunning people—to see if any-body was watching, any journalist, any photographer. There was nobody, so she walked away.

But a small hare was hiding in a bush. He said, "Aun-ty, what happened?"

The fox puffed her chest up as big as she could and said, "Nothing. Those grapes are not worthwhile. They are not ripe yet—they are sour."

Why should you write: *Who wants to be a man?*

Deep down somewhere you must be hankering to be a man. Every man wants to be a woman, every woman wants to be a man, for the simple reason that every man is both—man/woman—and every woman is both —woman/man. You are born out of the meeting of male and female energies; half of you belongs to your father and half of you belongs to your mother. You are a meeting of two polar opposites, two energies.

The only difference between man and woman is this: that the woman has the consciousness of a woman and the unconscious of a man, and the man has the con-sciousness of a man and the unconscious of a woman. But *both* are both!

That's why it is possible to be homosexuals, lesbians; otherwise it would be impossible. This phenomenon has been happening down the ages; it is nothing new. The reason is simple: because the man is only half man and half woman; the woman part is hidden deep in the darkness. But the conscious part can become tired, and when the conscious part becomes tired the uncon-scious takes over. Hence he may have the body of a man, but he starts functioning like a woman. And the same happens to a lesbian: on the surface she is a woman, but deep down the unconscious male energy has taken possession. Things have become upside-down. It will affect her physiology too.

There are a few lesbians here. Their physiology is bound to be affected by their psychology, because psychology and physiology are not two separate phenomena; they are joined together. Mind and body are not two; you are mindbody. So whatsoever happens in your physiology affects your psychology. That's why hormones can be given to you and your psychology can be changed. Now we know a man can be changed into a woman, a woman can be changed into a man.

And this is *my* observation: that in the coming century millions of people will change their sex. That will become something avant-garde; that will become something very progressive. That will be a new kind of freedom. Why remain confined to being a man your whole life when you can have both the worlds? If you can afford it you can change your sex. For a few years you remain a man and you look at the world from the male's viewpoint, and then you go for a simple operation and you are changed into a woman; now you can look at the world through the feminine eyes. And it is possible that a man may change many times. If the process becomes simpler, and it *will* become simpler—that's the whole work of science: to make things simpler and simpler—if the process becomes very simple, millions of people are bound to change.

It will release a great freedom in the world, but a great confusion also, a great chaos also. One day suddenly your husband comes home and he is a woman! Or your wife returns from a holiday and she is no more a woman. . . .

Because each is both, the desire to be the other is in everybody. Judy, it must be there and very insistently

there. Hence you are writing: *Who wants to be a man?*
Judy wants to be a man! I don't know about anybody
else. . . .

And you ask me: *Bhagwan, I am totally upset.*

That's good! So I am succeeding! I want you to be completely uprooted, upset, disturbed. I want to create a
chaos in you, because only out of chaos are stars born.

You ask me: *How can you talk nonsense?*

What else?! Sense cannot be talked . . . only nonsense
is left. So I don't take it as a criticism—it is a compli-
ment! Many many thanks to you. At least you are talking some sense!

You say: *My mind is having a fit and so is my
heart. What to do?*

I don't think anything can be done now. It is too late.
You *can't* go back—I will haunt you!—you can only go
ahead. Drop all these ideas that you are carrying within
yourself, this antagonism about men. Drop all these
ideas! I am neither for men nor for women. I am only
for transcendence.

And don't take my jokes seriously! You are such
fools that you can't even take jokes playfully. Another
woman has written: "Bhagwan, you have been talking
too much against women. The other day you called
them 'big-mouths'." Now this woman simply proves
that she is a big-mouth, nothing else! Nobody else has
felt offended. A joke is a joke! But why are you so
touchy? Now this woman must have a big mouth. At
least her husband must be telling her again and again,
"You big-mouth, shut up!" And now she comes here

to hear something beautiful said about her, and I tell a joke . . . and again that big mouth comes in.

Don't take jokes seriously. In fact, don't take anything seriously. You miss the point if you start taking things seriously. Even scriptures have to be taken non-seriously; only then can you understand. Understanding has to be with a deep, relaxed, non-serious, playful attitude. When you become serious you become tense. When you become serious you become closed. When you are playful many things can happen because in playfulness is creativity. In playfulness you can innovate.

But your ideas are continuously there; you can't put them aside.

Judy, now nothing can be done. You are a sannyasin. Now, being a sannyasin means you are neither man nor woman. Finished—that game is finished!

The third question

Bhagwan,
Aren't all people really the same?

Sudarsho,

SSENTIALLY YES, BUT ACCIDENTALLY NO. At the center yes, on the circumference no. Essentially we are made of the same stuff called God, but on the circumference God comes in every shape and size, in every color, in every form. There is much difference. And it is beautiful because if people were really the same, both at the center and on the circumference, the world would be a very boring place. But it is not a boring place. It is immensely interesting; it is immensely beautiful, rich. And the richness comes because of variety.

No two persons are the same on the circumference, although everybody is the same at the center—not only people but trees and rocks, they are also the same at the center. Call that center the soul and it will be easier for you to understand. Our souls are the same, there we meet and are one, but our bodies and minds are different, there we are separate.

And no effort should be made to make us similar on the surface. Down the ages people have been trying to do that; that creates only fascism. That's what Adolf Hitler was trying to do. That's what happens in every army: we try to make people similar even on the surface. In the army names disappear, numbers take their place. If a person dies you read on the board, "Number 14 has fallen." Now, number 14 has no personality. Anybody can replace number 14, anybody can be given number 14; number 14 is replaceable. But the person who has died, is he replaceable? Can anybody in the world ever replace him? Who will be the husband of his wife and who will be the father of his children? And who will be the son of his old parents? And who will be the friend of his friends? Number 14 cannot do that. Number 14 is perfectly okay in the army; he will carry the gun and he will do the same things—the same stupid things—that the other number 14 was doing before. But as far as their real personality is concerned, number 14 is a different person.

All the military leaders of the world have been trying to force a certain pattern on people. They would like machines, not men. They would like God to make men the way Ford cars are made, on an assembly line, so similar Fords go on coming. God does not work with an assembly line; he creates each individual with uniqueness.

So, Sudarsho, you have to understand two things. One: the variety, the difference, and love the variety and love the difference. . . .

Mohammedans have been trying to convert the whole world to one religion; Hindus have been trying to do the same, Christians have been doing the same, Buddhists have been doing the same. The whole effort is to make all the world similar, so there are all Christians and Christians. It will be a poor world where no temple exists and no mosque, where there are only churches and churches, and the same prayer and the same scripture and the same silly Pope. . .it won't be good! It is beautiful that there are three hundred religions in the world; more are needed.

In my vision, each person should have his own religion. There should be as many religions as there are people. Only then this conflict, this continuous conflict, will stop, this fight between religions will stop: when everybody has a religion and it is something unique like your signature, like the print of your thumb—unique. Then there will be no problem, no conflict; nobody will try to convert anybody. You don't try to convert people saying, "Make your signature just as I do." In fact, if somebody does it you will inform the police: "This man is trying to imitate me."

Religion should be a personal, intimate phenomenon. But there are people who want to change the whole world into Christianity or communism. They want to make the whole world Catholic or Mohammedan or Hindu.

Mohammedans say there is only one God and only

one prophet of God, that is Mohammed. Then God
seems to be very poor—just *one* prophet? Can't he
create more prophets? Mohammed has not exhausted
all the possibilities; nobody can exhaust them, neither
Buddha nor Jesus. They are all unique peaks, but no
peak can exhaust all the peaks. The Himalayas have
their own beauty, but it is different from the beauty of
the Alps; and the Alps have their own beauty, but it is
different from the beauty of the Vindhyas. Each mountain has its own beauty, each peak has its own beauty,
and it contributes to the richness of the world.

I would not like all people to become Christians or
Hindus or Mohammedans. I would like everybody to
be free from these prisons, everybody to be just
himself. This is a fascist idea, that everybody should be
like everybody else. And this fascist idea is being imposed in different ways on different aspects of humanity.

The heterosexuals will not allow anybody to be
homosexual. Why? Who are you to decide? Who has
given you the right to decide? If two persons are feeling
joyous in being homosexual, it is nobody else's business to interfere. But every society interferes.

Just the other day Aditya said Hamid had suggested
that there was no reason why he should not think of
turning into a gay person. Hamid must have joked. And
when I talked about it Hamid was very much disturbed: "What will people think about me now?" He
must have been joking with Aditya. Now he is very
much disturbed about his reputation. And of course, he
is our Ayatollah Hamidullah Kho-maniac! So his prestige. . . . Even Divya wept when she heard that Hamid
had invited Aditya! He must have been joking because
Iranians are very much against homosexuality.

In Iran, the punishment for homosexuality is death —although because of this punishment, more Iranians are homosexual than anybody else. Because when something is so dangerous, people become interested: "Naturally there must be something in it. When the punishment is death, that means there must be something higher than life in it, more than life in it. It is worth taking the risk!"

But why should people be worried about others? About everything the society remains alert: nobody should have his own individual way about his sex, about his love, about his clothes, about his way of talking, manners. Every society imposes a fascist rule on its members. It destroys much that is beautiful.

Sudarsho, you ask me: *Aren't all people really the same?*

Not as you know them.

The pretty co-ed nervously asked the doctor to perform an unusual operation: the removal of a large chunk of green wax from her navel.

Looking up from the ticklish task, the physician asked, "How did this happen?"

"Well, you see, doc," said the girl, "my boyfriend likes to eat by candlelight."

Nothing is wrong in it. This should be nobody else's business. If somebody wants to eat by candlelight he should be allowed. And where can you put the candle? The best place seems to be the navel—so natural. Some idea!

Abe and Mel talked of their no-account sons.

Abe said, "My no-good son. I give him a job in my

clothing business. I give him $50,000 a year, a new car, a beautiful apartment, and what does he do? He stays up all hours of the night, comes into work eleven or twelve o'clock and plays around with the models all afternoon.''

"You think you've got trouble?" Mel said. "My no-good son is worse. I give him a job in my clothing business. I pay him $50,000 a year and give him a new car and a beautiful apartment, and what does he do? He stays up all hours of the night, comes in eleven or twelve o'clock and plays around with the models all afternoon!''

"What's worse about that?" Abe questioned.

"You forget," Mel replied. "I am in men's clothing!''

On the circumference people are different, and they *should* be different, and everybody should maintain his individuality on the circumference. One should never compromise for any reason. Then only can we create a really democratic world. Real democracy means that the mob, the crowd, is no more in control of the individual life.

Democracy is less a political phenomenon than a religious phenomenon; it is far more important than politics. Democracy is a totally new vision of life. It has not yet happened anywhere; it has yet to happen. Democracy means each individual has the right to live according to his light; he should not be prevented. Unless he becomes a disturbance or a nuisance to others he should be allowed every freedom in all the aspects of life.

That's my vision of a really democratic world. That's how I would like my sannyasins to function: no interference in anybody's life. A great respect has to be given to the other.

But at the center, everybody is the same. When you meditate you move towards the center. In the deepest moments of meditation, all differences disappear. You are universal there, not individual.

And you have to be both: individual and universal. And you have to be very flexible and fluid between these two. It should be as easy as when you come out of your home, out of your house. When it is too cold inside you come out, you sit in the sun. When it becomes too hot you go in. It creates no problem; you just go in, you come out. There is no problem—it is your house.

A person should be capable of living on the circumference and at the center easily. He should be able to move from the marketplace to the meditative space and from the meditative space to the marketplace— with no problem, playfully, easily, spontaneously.

The fourth question

Bhagwan,
Most of my early life was spent in deadening myself to unbearable punishment. The deadening was entirely necessary for me to survive those times, but those days no longer exist, and after thirty-two years I am terrified and lack the courage to go within.
From where is the source of forgiveness, and, Bhagwan, what kind of foolish name have you given me?

Devaprem,

ALL NAMES ARE FOOLISH. That's why I have to explain the name to you, so at least it looks as if it is not foolish. I have to give it a beautiful meaning... otherwise names are names! They are just labels. "Devaprem" means divine love. What a beautiful name I have given to you! But, still, names are names.

There is an ancient Chinese ceremony in which the parents of a child choose the baby's name: as soon as the baby is born, all the cutlery in the house of its parents is thrown in the air. The parents then listen to the falling knives, forks, and spoons and choose a name —Ping, Chang, Tang, Fung, Chung....

That's also perfectly right! That seems to be a wise way to find out the name, as if God himself has chosen. And that's how *I* go on choosing your names. Do you think there is much esoteric, secret knowledge behind it? Nothing of the sort! Just anything, and I make a name out of it. I don't even think twice.

But I can understand why you feel that the name does not fit you. You have become a closed person and love has become difficult. It happens to many people—in fact, to the majority of people, more or less.

The child has to become unloving, unspontaneous. He has to deaden his sensitivity just to survive—*every* child, more or less; the difference is only of degrees. Every child has to learn tricks to survive. And the basic trick is: never be spontaneous. Be formal, never be natural, because your spontaneity is bound to be punished and your formality praised, rewarded.

The parents enforce a subtle strategy: they create fear

in the child if he says the truth. Nobody wants the child to say the truth, and the child is not yet capable of lying. But he has to learn.

When Cleo's parents threatened to forbid her to see her boyfriend unless she told them why he had been there so late the night before, she began to talk.

"Well, I took him . . . him into the loving room, and . . . ."

"That is *living,* dear," said the mother.

"You're telling me!"

Children are careful watchers, observers of what is happening all around. Of course, their senses are very clear, unclouded. They see the truth immediately. You cannot cheat a child; he knows it immediately, intuitively. And he is so innocent that it is impossible for him to be formal. But he has to be formal to survive. And man's child is very helpless. It is because of man's child's helplessness that our whole civilization exists. We can manage, mold the child in every possible way, whatsoever way we want.

Children are not supposed to say things that they know. They know much more than they ever tell you. They pretend to be innocent because you don't want them to know more than is taught in the school, than is taught by the preacher, than is taught by you; and they certainly know more. They move in society, in life, with keen, alert senses. They are watching everything, whatsoever is happening all around. But they learn one thing sooner or later: that they have to be diplomatic—with the grown-ups you can't be true, honest, sincere.

Three young French boys were spending the summer in the country. One afternoon they were strolling

through a field when they happened to see a couple lying under a tree, locked in a loving embrace.

"Mon dieu," exclaimed the youngest boy, who was
only six, "those people are having a terrible fight."

"But no, mon petit," replied the more sophisticated
nine-year-old, "those people are making love."

"True," agreed the oldest boy, a lad of eleven years,
"but what amateurs!"

But children cannot say these things to their parents
or before their parents. They know much more than
you think they know. They are so alert, so available to
life. They are so open and vulnerable; they go on
allowing every sensation to reach into their being. But
they have to deaden themselves sooner or later; they
have to become stiff, they have to become closed.
They learn one thing: that unless they follow their
parents, their priests, their politicians, they will have to
suffer much. Respectability is only for those who are
obedient.

> Devaprem, you say: *Most of my early life was
> spent in deadening myself to unbearable
> punishment. The deadening was entirely
> necessary for me to survive those times, but
> those days no longer exist, and after thirty-
> two years, I am terrified and lack the
> courage to go within.*

Now there is no need to be terrified; that has to be
understood. You can snap out of it! It is just an old
habit. A little intelligence . . . and that much intelligence everyone has. If you had the intelligence in
childhood to deaden yourself to survive, you *are* an intelligent person.

Now, the parents are not there . . . nobody is forcing anything on you, nobody is punishing you. It is just an old fear, a memory. You can snap out of it!

You don't need primal therapy: to go screaming against your parents for three years. That is not going to help—that is simply stupid. If it takes three years to shout and scream at your parents, and only then will you come out of it, that means you don't have any intelligence. And what is the guarantee that just by screaming for three years and shouting at your parents you will become intelligent? I think you will be less intelligent than you were before—three years of screaming and shouting? You will lose any intelligence that is left by your parents in you! There is no need! One has simply to see that those days are over. Meditation is enough.

Meditation means *seeing,* becoming aware, that those days are over, the fear is no more there, nobody is going to punish you. It is just an old habit. Snap out of it with as little fanfare as possible. Don't make much fuss about it. Because you make much fuss about it so many therapies have evolved. They are just aids for you so that you can make a fuss scientifically, so that your fuss is rationalized. But they are not needed by intelligent people.

An intelligent person is one who can see that it is no more night, it is day. Why are you afraid of darkness? Do you need first to scream for three hours against the night and the dark and the fear? That will be utterly stupid! That will destroy the day. Why waste it? The night is no more.

That's why in the East we have not developed any therapeutic methods like the West, for the simple reason that we came to understand one thing: that all that is needed is a little intelligence—and everybody has it. And meditation helps the intelligence to become sharp.

Just seeing is enough; seeing brings transformation. And when transformation comes without any long process it is far deeper. When it takes a long process that means it will remain superficial.

So I have not come across a single person yet whose primal therapy has totally succeeded. It can *never* succeed. Psychoanalysis has not been able to create a single person who is totally psychoanalyzed; even Sigmund Freud was not in that totality. Janov is not really what he is talking about—the primal man, the primal innocence—he is not. You can see in his face all kinds of tension, anguish, anxiety; it is so apparent. He needs a few more years of screaming; and then too I don't think those tensions will disappear. They may even become more subtle, more nourished, because if you scream for years, remember, you are practicing it; it is a kind of practice, a kind of cultivation of it. Then you become addicted to it; without screaming for a few hours you won't feel good. Then it is an intoxicating process, a kind of auto-hypnosis. Yes, screaming for one hour every day will make you feel a little relaxed, but it is a stupid kind of relaxation.

Seeing is transformation. That is our experience in the East. All the Buddhas in the East have given only one meditation: watchfulness, awareness.

Now, Devaprem, you know, you are aware of how this fear has arisen in you: out of thirty years of fear, continuous fear of punishment, you have become closed, encapsulated, and you are always on guard. You cannot relax, you cannot be true, you cannot be honest. You cannot say the thing that you want to say, you cannot do the thing that you always wanted to do. You *know*—and now. . . .

It was right in those years—you behaved intelligently. Nothing was wrong, otherwise you would not have survived. Now you have survived, get out of it—it is no more needed. The disease is no more, why go on carrying the bottles of medicines and prescriptions? Do you need a therapy to throw the bottles and the prescriptions? Will you go to a therapist and say, "Now the disease is no more, but I can't let go of this prescription. I go on carrying it, and these bottles. I don't need them any more. How to drop them?" Is any "how" needed? No "how" is needed. Go to the Rotary Club and donate them! They collect medicines, etcetera, which are not needed by anybody else. Their motto is: We serve. So help them serve people.

It is very simple to come out. But why do people make so much out of it?—because that is part of your ego. You don't want it to be so simple. Thirty years of life—and I am making a joke of it! You would like to pay some therapist good money and you would like to invest some time. That feels good; it makes you feel important.

In fact, in the West now people brag that they have been in psychoanalysis for three years or seven years. And somebody else brags that "Psychoanalysis is out of date. I have been in gestalt therapy, in primal therapy." And there are "groupies" now who go on moving from one group to another group. Their whole life consists of moving from one group to another group.

Many groupies come to me and they say, "We have done *all* the groups." And they say it in the same way as in the old days people used to say, "We have fasted, prayed, and we have sacrificed all our joys, and we are saints"—in the same way! This is a new kind of holiness that is arising in the world: "I have passed through all kinds of groups." And I look in their eyes and they say, "And nothing has happened."

They are saying, "My problems are far more complex, far more deep-rooted than these therapies can go. They can't help me. I am no *ordinary* person; my problems are extraordinary."

People enjoy saying it. I see a light in their eyes when they say, "Nobody has been able to help me. Bhagwan, can *you* help me?" They are giving me a challenge! All that they want is to add one more name to their list: "I have been to this guy too and he cannot help. My problems are such . . . not ordinary problems that anybody can help."

People brag about their diseases too, remember. They may just have some ordinary disease, but who wants to have some ordinary disease?

Have you ever watched your own reaction? When you go to the doctor with a throbbing heart, thinking it is cancer, and he says,"It is nothing.It is just a common cold" . . . have you observed?—you feel a little sad. Just a common cold? A desire arises to visit another doctor. *you* and a common cold?! You are not a common person, how can you have a common cold? Ego is such that it thrives on every kind of thing, right or wrong.

So don't be much worried about it. It is past, it is finished. Slip out of it—and without making any noise, without making any ceremony that you are getting out of it. Just start being again alive, sensitive, as you had always been in your childhood. That is your nature so it can be reclaimed easily. What you have learned is not your nature so it can be unlearned very easily.

The last question

Bhagwan,
Are all the journalists blind? Can't they see the
truth? Why are they continuously spreading
lies about you?

Nisha,

THE PROFESSION OF A JOURNALIST is such that it lives on lies. Truth is not news; lies are news, beautiful news. The bigger the lie the better the news, because it has a certain quality in it: the quality of creating a sensation. Journalism lives on lies. If journalists decide only to be true, there won't be so many newspapers, so many magazines. And there will not be much news either. Truth you can write on a postcard.

I have heard that in heaven there are no newspapers because no news ever happens there.

George Bernard Shaw has made a definition: "When a dog bites a man it is not news, but when a man bites a dog it is news." In heaven no man bites a dog. In the first place it is very difficult to find a dog there; in the second place nobody is interested in biting anybody, so what news can you have?

But in hell they have really great newspapers and there circulation is in the millions. They have news there. Every day, every moment, things are happening —everybody is biting everybody else.

When journalists come they come to find something sensational. If they cannot find it they have to invent it; otherwise their coming and going has been useless. And if a journalist goes back to his office without any news again and again, his job is gone. Either find something sensational or invent it.

Journalism depends on invention. And then slowly slowly a journalist starts having a certain kind of approach towards things: he immediately sees the negative. He can't see the positive because the positive is not his business.

It is like a shoemaker: he looks only at your shoes, not at your face. What does he have to do with your face? In fact, looking at your shoe he knows your whole biography; a real shoemaker just looking at your shoe can say everything about your life far more accurately than any astrologer can. The condition of the shoe will show the condition, the financial condition, in which you are. If you have to walk too much, that will show that you don't have a car, that you don't have any money. The shoe will say so many things. The shoemaker looks only at the shoe, and the tailor looks only at your clothes, and the doctor looks only at the diseases. Bring a perfectly healthy man to a doctor and you will be surprised: he will find many diseases.

I have heard that one doctor friend of Picasso had come to visit him. Picasso had just finished a portrait. He invited the doctor friend to see the portrait. He looked; he looked from this side and from that side, and then he asked for a torch—in the daytime!

Picasso was puzzled, but he was intrigued also so he gave him a torch. He looked into the eyes of the portrait and he said, "Pneumonia."

A doctor is a doctor! His profession gives him a certain eye.

The journalist comes here with a certain eye, with certain fixed ideas, prejudices. He comes to pick up on something negative which can become sensational. And then, of course, he can find it; and if he cannot find it he can invent it. And they look only from the outside; they are too afraid to get involved deeper. A few journalists have got involved—once they get involved they are no more journalists.

You can ask Satyananda. He was a famous journalist in one of the most important magazines in Germany, *Stern.* He got so much involved . . . he didn't function here like a journalist. He tried to know things from the inside. He participated in groups, in meditations, and then . . . he became a sannyasin.

Stern refused to publish his story because they said, "You are no more a journalist. Now you have become part of this orange movement, so whatsoever you say will be favorable."

For months he had to insist, "I have worked hard!" They cut his story almost by half. They destroyed his whole story, distorted the whole story, and only then did they print it. And he lost his job!

Now he has come here forever. There are a few other journalists also, at least a dozen. Subhuti is here and others are here. . . .

A journalist is taught by his profession to always remain at a distance: "Look from the outside." And from the outside you can never know how things are.

A pretty young woman was traveling in a train across Texas. A dapper looking man walked up to her and whispered something in her ear, whereupon she gave him a stinging slap in the face.

A tall Texan seated across the aisle stood up and asked her, "Is this man molesting you, Ma'am?"

"He certainly is," she replied. "He just offered me ten dollars if I would go with him to his sleeping compartment."

Without hesitation, the Texan pulled out his pistol
and shot the man.

"Good God!" cried the woman. "That's no reason
to kill him!"

"I will kill any man," replied the Texan, "who tries
to raise the prices in Texas."

If you had looked only from the outside you would
never have thought about this, what was inside the
mind of the Texan. You would have thought him a
great saint or something.

But the journalist has to keep a distance. He thinks
that by keeping a distance he will be able to know better. No, he will only gather information, bits of information, in fact irrelevant, unconnected with each
other, because he has no approach to the center. And
he is going to distort it more to make it more sensational.

A group of Rajneesh sannyasins in Bonn, Germany,
were taking a boatride down the Rhine river when they
noticed that a well-known journalist was aboard the
boat. They decided to do something to give sannyasins
a more positive image in Germany. So, before the eyes
of the journalist, they stepped off into the water and
did a whirling Sufi dance all the way around the moving boat. Then, completely dry, they climbed back onto the boat's deck.

The next day the sannyasins eagerly scanned the
newspaper to see what the journalist had written about
their fantastic feat.

There, in the back pages, they found a small article
with the headline: WHEN WILL RAJNEESH SANNYASINS
FINALLY LEARN TO SWIM?

DOGO HAD A DISCIPLE *called Soshin. When Soshin was taken in as a novice, it was perhaps natural of him to expect lessons in Zen from his teacher the way a schoolboy is taught at school. But Dogo gave him no special lessons on the subject, and this bewildered and disappointed Soshin.*

One day he said to the Master, "It is some time since I came here, but not a word has been given me regarding the essence of the Zen teaching."

Dogo replied, "Since your arrival I have ever been giving you lessons on the matter of Zen discipline."

"What kind of lesson could it have been?"

"When you bring me a cup of tea in the morning, I take it; when you serve me a meal, I accept it; when you bow to me, I return it with a nod. How else do you expect to be taught in the discipline of Zen?"

Soshin hung his head for a while, pondering the puzzling words of the Master.

The Master said, "If you want to see, see right at once. When you begin to think, you miss the point."

See Right
at Once

Sujata has written to me:

*How odd
of God
to choose
the Jews!*

Sujata,

GOD HAS A TREMENDOUS SENSE OF HUMOR! Religion remains something dead without a sense of humor as a foundation to it. God would not have been able to create the world if he had no sense of humor. God is not serious at all. Seriousness is a state of dis-ease; humor is health. Love, laughter, life, they are aspects of the same energy.

But for centuries people have been told that God is very serious. These people were pathological. They created a serious God, they projected a serious God, out of their own pathology. And we have worshipped these people as saints. They were not saints. They needed great awakening; they were fast asleep in their seriousness. They needed laughter—that would have helped them more than all their prayers and fasting; that would have cleansed their souls in a far better way than all their ascetic practices. They did not need more scriptures, more theologies; they needed only the capacity to laugh at the beautiful absurdity of life. It is ecstatically absurd. It is not a rational phenomenon; it is utterly irrational.

Moses went up the mountain. After a long time God appeared. "Hello, Moses. Good to see you. Sorry you had to wait, but I think you will feel it was worth it because I have something very special for you today."

Moses thought for a second and then said, "Oh, no, Lord, really. Thank you, but I don't need anything right now. Some other time perhaps."

"Moses, this is free," said the Lord.

"Then," said Moses, "give me ten!"

That's how the Jews got the Ten Commandments.

Sujata, Zen has something Jewish in it. It is really very puzzling why Zen did not appear in the Jewish world. But the Chinese also have a tremendous sense of humor. Zen is not Indian, remember. Of course, the origin is in Gautam the Buddha, but it went through a tremendous transformation passing through the Chinese consciousness.

There are a few very wise people who think that Zen is more a rebellion against the Indian seriousness than a continuity of it. And they have a point there; a certain truth is there. Lao Tzu is more Jewish than Hindu—he can laugh. Chuang Tzu has written such beautiful and absurd stories; nobody can conceive of an enlightened person writing such stories, which can only be called, at the best, entertainment. But entertainment can become the door to enlightenment.

Zen is originally connected with Buddha, but the color and the flavor that came to it came through Lao Tzu, Chuang Tzu, Lieh Tzu and the Chinese consciousness. And then it blossomed in Japan; it came to its ultimate peak in Japan. Japan also has a great quality: of taking life playfully. The consciousness of Japan is very colorful.

Zen could have happened in the Jewish world too. Something like it really *did* happen—that is Hassidism. This story must have come from Jewish sources, although it is about Jesus. But Christians have no sense of humor. And Jesus was never a Christian, remember. He was born a Jew, he lived as a Jew, he died as a Jew.

Jesus is hanging on the cross singing, "Da-di-li-da-dum-dei. . . . ."

Suddenly Peter hisses from underneath, "Hey, Jesus!"

Jesus goes on, "Da-li-di-dum-da-dum-da-dei . . ."

Peter, now more urgently, "Hey, Jesus, stop it!"

Jesus continues happily with "Di-duah-duah. . . . ."

Finally Peter yells, "For God's sake, Jesus, cut it out! Tourists are coming!"

Try to understand Zen through laughter, not through prayer. Try to understand Zen through flowers, butterflies, sun, moon, children, people in all their absurdities. Watch this whole panorama of life, all these colors, the whole spectrum.

Zen is not a doctrine, it is not a dogma. It is growing into an insight. It is a vision—very light-hearted, not serious at all.

Be light-hearted, light-footed. Be of light step. Don't carry religion like a burden. And don't expect religion to be a teaching; it is not. It is certainly a discipline, but not a teaching at all. Teaching has to be imposed upon you from the outside and teaching can only reach to your mind, never to your heart, and never, never to the very center of your being. Teaching remains intellectual. It is an answer to human curiosity, and curiosity is not a true search.

The student remains outside the temple of Zen because he remains curious. He wants to know answers and there are none. He has some stupid questions to be answered: "Who made the world? Why did he make the world?" And so on and so forth. "How many heavens are there and how many hells? And how many angels can dance on the point of a needle? And is the world infinite or finite? Are there many lives or only one?" These are all curiosities—good for a student of philosophy but not good for a disciple.

A disciple has to drop curiosity. Curiosity is something very superficial. Even if those questions are answered, nothing will have happened to your being; you will remain the same. Yes, you will have more information, and out of that information you will create new questions. Each question answered brings ten more new questions; the answer creates ten more new questions.

If somebody says, "God created the world," then the question is, "Why did he create the world? And why a world like this?—so miserable. If he is omnipotent, omniscient, omnipresent, could he not see what he was doing? Why did he create pain, disease, death?" Now, so many questions. . . .

Philosophy is an exercise in futility.

A student comes out of curiosity. Unless he becomes a disciple he will not become aware that curiosity is a vicious circle. You ask one question, you are given the answer, the answer brings ten more new questions, and so on and so forth. And the tree becomes bigger and bigger; thicker and thicker is the foliage. And finally the philosopher has only questions and no answers at all.

Surrounded by all those stupid questions . . . stupid I call them because they have no answers; stupid I call them because they are born out of childish curiosity. When one is surrounded by all those questions and there is no answer, one loses sharpness, one loses clarity, one is clouded. And one is no more intelligent. The more intellectual one becomes, the less intelligent he is.

The professor who had committed his wife to a mental institution was talking to the chief of staff. "How will we know when my wife is well again, doctor?"

"We have a simple test we give all our patients," he replied. "We put a hose into a trough, turn on the water, give the patient a bucket, and tell him to empty out the trough."

"What does that prove?" enquired the professor.

"Elementary, sir," the doctor assured him. "Any sane person will turn off the hose."

Isn't science wonderful!" he replied. "I never would have thought of that!"

He must be a professor of philosophy; he can't be less than that.

The professor only knows questions. He is lost in the jungle of questions. The philosopher remains immature. Maturity is of consciousness, not of intellectuality. It is not of knowledge, it is of innocence.

Yes: *Not to know is the most intimate.* And to function out of that not-knowing is to function in an enlightened way. To respond out of not-knowing is to respond like a Buddha. That is true response because it is not clouded, not distorted, not contaminated, not polluted and poisoned by your mind and your past. It is fresh, it is young, it is new. It arises to the challenge of the present. It is always in synchronicity with the new, with the present. And the present is always new, it is always moving—it is dynamic. All your answers are static, and life is dynamic.

HENCE ZEN IS NOT INTERESTED IN ANSWERS—or in questions. It is not interested in teaching at all. It is not a philosophy; it is a totally different way of looking at things, at life, at existence, at oneself, at others. Yes, it is a discipline.

Discipline simply means a methodology of becoming more centered, of becoming more alert, of becoming more aware, of bringing more meditativeness to your being; not functioning through the head, not even through the heart, but functioning from the very core of your being, from the very innermost core, from the center of your being, from your totality. It is not a reaction—reaction comes from the past—it is a response. Response is always *in* the present, *to* the present.

Zen gives you a discipline to become a mirror so that you can reflect that which is. All that is needed is a thoughtless awareness.

The first thing to be dropped is curiosity, because curiosity will keep you tethered to the futile. It will keep you being a student; it will never allow you to become a disciple.

Boris, who was from Russia, had been in America only a few months. He did not speak English very well.

One day he was asked, "Boris, what is it that you are most anxious to see in America?"

"Well," replied Boris, "I weesh most to meet the most famous Mrs. Beech, who had so many sons in the last war."

Get it? He must have heard all the Americans calling each other "sonofabitch, sonofabitch. . . " so he is very much interested, anxious, curious, to know about Mrs. Beech, the famous Mrs. Beech.

Curiosity is always like that. It is foolish, but it can keep you tethered to the mind. And don't think that there is some curiosity which is spiritual, metaphysical. No, nothing like that exists; all curiosity is the same. Whether you enquire about "the famous Mrs. Beech" or you enquire about God it is all the same. Enquiry from the mind will have the same quality—of childishness.

There is a totally different kind of enquiry that arises from the deeper recesses of your being.

Zen is interested in discipline, not in teaching. It wants you to be more alert so you can see more clearly. It does not give you the answer; it gives you the *eyes* to see. What is the use of telling a blind man what light is and all the theories about light? It is futile. You are simply being stupid by answering the curiosity of a blind man. What is urgently needed is treatment of his eyes. He needs an operation, he needs new eyes, he needs medicine. That is discipline.

Buddha has said: "I am a physician, not a philosopher." And Zen is absolutely a treatment. It is the greatest treatment that has come to humanity, out of the work

of thousands of enlightened people—very refined. It
can help to open up your eyes. It can help you to feel
again, to be sensitive to the reality. It can give you eyes
and ears. It can give you a soul. But it is not interested
in answers.

Meditate over this beautiful story:

*Dogo had a disciple called Soshin. When Soshin was
taken in as a novice, it was perhaps natural of him
to expect lessons in Zen from his teacher the way
a schoolboy is taught at school.*

YES, IT IS NATURAL IN A WAY, because that's how we
are conditioned. Knowledge is given to us in the
form of questions and answers. From the primary
school to the university that's how we are taught, conditioned, hypnotized. And naturally, after one third of
your life is wasted in that way, you become accustomed to it. Then you start asking profound questions
in the same way as one asks, "How much is two plus
two?" You start asking about love, life, God, meditation—in the same way!

In fact, even that ordinary question is not answerable. If you ask the real mathematicians, even this simple question "How much is two plus two?" is not
answerable, because sometimes it is five and sometimes
it is three. It is very rarely four. It is an exception that
two plus two comes to be four, very exceptional, for
the simple reason that two things are never the same. It
is an abstraction: you add two and two and you say
four.

Two persons and two persons are four *different* persons, *so* different that you cannot create an abstraction

out of them. Even two leaves and two other leaves are so different that you cannot simply call them four leaves; they are not the same. Their weights are different, their colors are different, their shapes are different, their tastes are different. No two things in the world are the same. So how can two plus two be four? It is just an abstraction; it is lower mathematics. Higher mathematics knows that this is only utilitarian, it is not a truth. Mathematics is an invention of man; it is a workable lie.

What to say about love, which goes beyond all mathematics and all logic? In love, one plus one becomes one, not two. In deep love, the twoness disappears. Mathematics is transcended; it becomes irrelevant. In deep love, two persons are no more two persons, they become one. They start feeling, functioning, as one unit, as one organic unity, as one orgasmic joy. Mathematics won't do, logic won't do, chemistry won't do, biology won't do, physiology won't do. Love is something which has to be experienced in a totally different way. It cannot be taught in the ordinary ways of teaching; it cannot become part of pedagogy.

But the disciple, Soshin, was a novice, a newcomer.

> *. . . it was perhaps natural of him to expect lessons in Zen from his teacher the way a schoolboy is taught at school.*

It is natural in a state of unconsciousness.

Remember, there are two natures. One is when you are asleep; then many things are natural. Somebody insults you, you become angry, and that is *natural*—but only in unconsciousness, in sleep. You insult the Buddha, he does not become angry—that is higher nature, a totally different kind of nature. He is functioning from a different center altogether. He may feel compassion for you, not anger. He functions through awareness, you function through unawareness.

In sleep you cannot do anything of any value, you cannot do anything valuable. Whatsoever you do is all dream. You imagine, you think you are doing good.

Just the other day somebody asked: "I want to do good, I want to *be* good. Bhagwan, help me."

I cannot help you directly to do good or to be good; I can help you only indirectly. I can help you only to be more meditative. And on the surface it may seem that your question is about something else and my answer is totally different: you want to be good and I talk about meditation. How are they related? If you are asleep you may *think* you are doing good, you may do harm. You may *think* you are doing harm, you may do good. In your sleep everything is possible.

You will become a do-gooder—and do-gooders are the most mischievous people. We have suffered much from these do-gooders. They don't know who they are, they don't know any silent state of consciousness, they are not aware, but they go on doing good. What to say about good? A sleepy person cannot even be certain of doing harm. He may think he is doing harm and the result may be totally different.

That's how acupuncture was discovered. A man wanted to kill somebody; he shot him with an arrow. And that man, the victim, had suffered his whole life from a headache. The arrow hit him on the leg and the headache disappeared, totally disappeared. He was puzzled.

He went to his physician saying, "You have not been able to treat me and my enemy has treated me. He wanted to kill me, but something went wrong—my headache has disappeared. I am grateful to him.''

Then the physicians started thinking about it, how it happened. That's what acupuncturists go on doing now.

You can go to Abhiyana. You may have a headache and he may start putting needles all over your body. Those needle points were discovered because of this accident. Five thousand years have passed; in these five thousand years acupuncture has developed tremendously. Now there is much scientific support for it.

In Soviet Russia they are working on acupuncture very seriously because it has great potential: it can cure almost all diseases. Those needles can change the currents of your body electricity.

That man must have suffered from too much electricity in the head. The arrow hit a certain meridian, a certain electric current in his leg, and the electricity changed its course; it was no longer going to the head. Hence the headache disappeared.

Now, the man who wanted to do harm did a great, beneficial act for the whole of humanity—not only for that man—because in these five thousand years, millions of people have been helped by acupuncture. The whole credit goes to that unknown person who wanted to kill.

In your unconsciousness it is difficult to decide what the outcome will be. You move in a dark dark night. All is accidental.

Sindenburg had lived a virtuous life; he was even president of the synagogue. But when he entered heaven the angel in charge said, ''You can't stay here.''

''Why?'' asked Sindenburg. ''I always tried to be a good man.''

"That is it," explained the angel. "Everyone here was a good man, but they all committed at least one sin. Since you didn't sin at all, the rest of the souls will resent you."

"But," protested Sindenburg, "isn't there something I can do?"

"Well," considered the angel, "you can have six more hours on earth to commit a sin, but you must do somebody a real injury."

Sindenburg went back to earth and suddenly he saw a middle-aged woman looking at him. They started talking; she invited him home with her. Soon they were making love like two teenagers.

Six hours later Sindenburg said, "I am sorry, but I have to go now."

"Listen!" cried the woman. "I never married or even had a man. You just gave me the best time I had in my whole life. What a good deed you did today!"

Now he came to do some real injury and what he has really done is a good deed. The woman is immensely happy and grateful. And those six hours are gone; now there is no more time left. Again he will be in trouble!

In sleep you cannot do good—you cannot even do bad! All is accidental. And when a person comes to a Master he comes almost fast asleep. He comes out of curiosity, accidentally. He expects much, and his expectations are natural in his state.

He expected *lessons in Zen*. . . .

Now that is absolutely foolish: there are no lessons in Zen. Zen, in the first place, is not a teaching but a device to awaken you. It is not information, it is not knowledge. It is a method to shake you up, to wake

you up. Teaching means you are fast asleep and somebody goes on talking about what awakening is—and
you go on snoring and he goes on talking. *You* are
asleep, *he* is asleep; otherwise he will not talk to you. At
least when he sees that you are snoring he will not talk
to you.

When I was a student at university I had a great
teacher, a very well-known philosopher. For three
years nobody had joined his class—he was the head of
the department. And people were afraid to join his class
because he was a non-stop talker. Sometimes two
hours, three hours, four hours. . . . And he had this
condition: he would say to every student, "If you want
to participate in *my* classes, if you want to take *my* subject, then this must be remembered: that I can *start* my
lecture when the period starts, but I cannot stop when
the period is over. Unless I am totally finished with the
subject . . . and how can it be managed within forty
minutes? Sometimes it takes two hours, sometimes it
takes only half an hour. So whenever it is finished, that
is the end."

He also told me the same. I wanted to join his class—
I was intrigued by the old man. He said, "Listen! Don't
blame me later on. Sometimes I speak for four hours;
five hours also I have spoken."

I said, "You don't be worried about that. I can speak
longer than you." And I told him, "Remember that
when I start speaking I forget who is the teacher and
who is the student. I don't care! So you also keep it in
mind that if *I* start speaking you cannot stop me.

"And secondly: the time of your periods is such that
those are the hours when I sleep. From twelve to two I
must sleep; that I have done my whole life. I can sleep

longer—I have slept from eleven to five, the whole day—but this much is absolutely necessary, that I cannot miss. So I will sleep—you can go on talking.''

He said, "How can you sleep when I am talking?"

I said, "I use earplugs! You go on talking. I am not concerned with your talk at all, that is up to you. You enjoy it to your heart's content—I will be sleeping. And you cannot object to that.''

He agreed to my condition, I agreed to his condition. And that's how we became great friends: he would speak and I would sleep.

Now this person must be fast asleep himself, otherwise why . . . because I was the only student in his class! To whom was he talking? He was unburdening himself. And he was very happy to find a student who would at least remain in the class—although asleep, but at least he was there.

This is what goes on in the whole world! Priests are asleep talking to their congregations. Professors are asleep talking to their students—metaphysically asleep; I am not talking about the ordinary sleep. Metaphysically everybody is snoring.

Zen is not a teaching, because it knows you are asleep. The primary thing is not to teach you; the primary thing is to wake you up. Zen is an alarm.

But Soshin naturally expected some lessons in Zen from his teacher *the way a schoolboy is taught at school.*

Remember, if Zen is not a teaching then you cannot call the Zen Master a teacher either. He is not a teacher, he is a Master. And there is a great difference between a teacher and a Master. But when you first come in close contact with a Master you think of him as a teacher—

maybe a great teacher, but still you think in terms of his being a teacher. And the reason is in your expectation that he is teaching something: that he is teaching great philosophy, that he is teaching great truths.

No, a real Master is not a teacher: a real Master is an awakener. His function is totally different from a teacher; his function is far more difficult. And only very few people can stay with a Master because to wake up after millions of lives is not an ordinary feat; it is a miracle. And to allow somebody to wake you up needs great trust, great surrender.

So in Zen, first, people are accepted only as novices, as beginners. Only when the Master sees some quality in them which can be awakened, when he sees something very potential, then they are accepted and initiated into higher things. Otherwise they remain novices for years, doing small things: cleaning the floor, cooking the food, chopping wood, carrying water from the well. And the Master goes on watching and he goes on helping them to become a little more alert while they are chopping wood, while they are carrying water from the well, while they are cleaning the floor.

You will see here in this commune at least one thousand sannyasins doing different kinds of things. When Indians come here for the first time they are puzzled, because their idea of an ashram, of a religious commune, is totally different. People should be sitting praying, doing *bhajan.* They can't conceive that people should be working, cooking food, weaving, doing pottery, painting, photography, creating music, poetry, dancing. They can't believe their eyes when they see the commune for the first time. They come with certain expectations. And they want you to look serious, religious, holy. And you look so joyous! You look so

loving, so warm. They expect you to be utterly cold—
as cold as corpses. And you are so warm and so loving
and so alive that they are shocked for the first time.

Zen does not believe that people should just live a
holy life, a virtuous life, doing nothing—just turning
beads or repeating some mantra. Zen believes in creativity. Zen believes in the ordinary world. It wants to
transform the mundane into the sacred.

So the first message given to the beginners is to start
work but be alert. And it is easier to be alert while you
are working than while you are simply chanting a mantra, because when you are chanting a mantra every
possibility is that the mantra will function as a tranquilizer. When you repeat a single word again and again it
creates sleep because it creates boredom. When you
repeat a certain word again and again it changes your
inner chemistry. It is one of the ancientmost ways of
falling asleep.

If you cannot fall asleep in the night, if you suffer
from sleeplessness, then methods like Maharishi
Mahesh Yogi's Transcendental Meditation are perfectly
good. That method has nothing to do with meditation;
it is neither meditation nor transcendental. It is simply a
non-medicinal tranquilizer. It is good as far as it can
bring sleep and without any drug—I appreciate it—but
it has nothing to do with meditation.

You can repeat your own name again and again and
you don't need to pay the fees to anybody and you
don't need any initiation. Just repeat your own name;
repeat it fast so that nothing else enters your mind, only your name resounds. Repeat loudly inside so that
from your toes to the head it is resounding inside. Soon
you will get bored, fed up. And that is the moment

when you start falling asleep because there seems to be
no other escape.

All mothers know it. It is one of the ancientmost
methods women have been using with their children,
on their children. They didn't call it Transcendental
Meditation; they used to call it "lullaby." The child
tosses and turns, but the mother goes on repeating the
same line again and again. And finding no other escape
outside, the child escapes inside; that means he falls
asleep. He says, "I am so fed up that unless I fall asleep,
this woman is not going to stop." And soon he learns:
the moment he falls asleep the woman stops, so it becomes a conditioning; then it becomes a conditioned
reflex. Slowly slowly, the woman just repeats the line
one or two times and the child is fast asleep.

This you can do to yourself. It is a process of auto-
hypnosis; good as far as sleep is concerned but it has
nothing to do with meditation. In fact, it is just the opposite of meditation, because meditation brings awareness and this method brings sleep. Hence I appreciate it
as a technique for sleep, but I am totally against it if it is
taught to people as a method of meditation.

> Soshin expected *lessons in Zen from his teacher
> the way a schoolboy is taught at school.*

This is *your* story. This is everybody's story. Each
seeker comes with such expectations.

Sometimes foolish people come to me and they ask:
"What is your teaching in short?" Which of your books
contains your total teaching?"

I have no teaching! That's why so many books are
possible. Otherwise how can so many books be possible? If you have a certain teaching, then one or two

books will do. That's why I can go on talking for ever, because I have no teaching. Every teaching will sooner or later be exhausted; I cannot be exhausted. There is no beginning and no end . . . we are always in the middle. I am not a teacher.

Everybody grows physically but psychologically remains a child. Your psychological age is never more than thirteen, even less than that. It was a shock when it was discovered for the first time in the First World War that man's average psychological age is only twelve or thirteen at the most. That means you may be seventy but your mind is only thirteen. So if somebody looks at your body you look so old, so experienced, but if somebody looks into your mind you are carrying the same childish mind still.

Your God is nothing but a projected father; it is a father fixation. You cannot live without the idea of a father. Maybe your actual father is dead and you cannot conceive of yourself without a father. You need an imaginary father in heaven who takes care of you, who looks after you. And, certainly, the ordinary father is bound to die one day or other so you need a heavenly father who is eternal, who will never die, so he will become your safety and security.

Once somebody asked George Gurdjieff, "Why do all the religions teach: Respect your parents?"

Gurdjieff said, "For a simple reason: if you respect your parents you will respect God, because God is nothing but the ultimate parent. If you don't respect your parents you will not be bothered with God either."

A great insight: God is the great father; you are just small children searching for a lost father, searching for a lost childhood, searching for the security of childhood. Your behavior is childish.

A young father was shopping at a department store with his daughter when the little girl suddenly said, "Daddy, I gotta go."

"Not right now," replied the father.

"I gotta go *now!*" shouted the girl.

To avoid a crisis a saleslady stepped up and said, "That's all right, sir, I will take her."

The saleslady and the little girl went off hurriedly, hand in hand. On their return, Tony looked at his daughter and said, "Did you thank the nice lady for being so kind?"

"Why should I thank her?" retorted the little girl. "She had to go too!"

Just watch your reactions and you will be surprised: they are childish. Your manners, howsoever sophisticated from the outside, deep down are childish. Your prayers, your church-going, are *all* childish.

Zen is not concerned with your childish state of mind. It has no desire to nourish it any more. Its concern is maturity; it wants you to become mature, it wants you to become ripe. Hence it has no idea of God —no father in the sky. It leaves you totally alone because only in aloneness is maturity possible. It leaves you totally in insecurity. It gives you no security, no guarantee. It gives you all kinds of insecurities to move into.

And that's what sannyas is also: a quantum leap into insecurity, a quantum leap into the unknown, because only with that encounter will you become mature. And maturity is freedom, maturity is liberation.

But Dogo gave him no special lessons on the
subject. . . .

There are none.

. . . and this bewildered and disappointed Soshin.

Naturally. He was expecting and expecting and waiting,
and no special lessons were given. He wanted a few
simple principles so he could cling to them, so that he
could hold onto them, so that they would become his
treasure, his knowledge. And the Master had not given
any special lesson. Naturally he was disappointed. If
you are expecting anything you are bound to be disappointed. Expectation always brings disappointment,
frustration.

One day he said to the Master, "It is some time since
I came here, but not a word has been given me
regarding the essence of the Zen teaching."

People are in a hurry. I have come to know people
who have meditated three days, and on the fourth day
they ask, "Three days we have been meditating, why
has nothing happened yet?"

As if they are obliging existence by meditating for so
long—three days, one hour every day; that means
three hours. And if you actually look, in their meditation they were just daydreaming; with closed eyes they
were daydreaming. They call it meditation! And just
because for three days they have been sitting for one
hour—with great difficulty, somehow managing, great
noise inside, no silence, no peace, no consciousness,
just desires, thoughts, memories, imagination, constant
traffic, a crowd—then they come on the fourth day

saying, "Bhagwan, what is happening? Three days have passed and nothing has happened yet."

Time should not be taken into account at all—three years, not even three lives. You should not think in terms of time, because the phenomenon of meditation is non-temporal. It can happen any moment, it can happen *right* now; it may take years, it may take lives. It all depends on your intensity, on your sincerity, and it all depends on your totality.

A pretty young woman stepped onto a crowded streetcar, and seeing that all the seats were taken she asked, "Would one of you gentlemen make room for a pregnant woman?"

A middle-aged man quickly stood up and gave her his seat. After she was seated he solicitously asked her, "How long have you been pregnant?"

"About fifteen minutes, and God, am I tired!"

Fifteen minutes pregnant! Even that is okay, but three days of meditation is even more stupid.

> *Soshin said one day to the Master. . . .*

There must be some anger, frustration, disappointment. Has he chosen a wrong person to be with? No special teaching has been given yet—and the ego always wants something special.

> *"It is some time since I came here," he said, "but not a word has been given me regarding the essence of the Zen teaching."*

In the first place, there is no Zen teaching as such. Zen is a method of awakening, not a theology. It does not talk about God: it forces you into God. It hits you in many ways so that you can be awakened into God. To be asleep is to be in the world: to be awake is to be in God. Methods are there, devices are there, but no teaching at all.

In a little New Mexico town, a pretty young tourist overheard a virile Navajo saying "Chance!" to every passing female.

Finally her curiosity got the better of her and she walked up to him and said "Hello," to which he answered "Chance!"

"I thought all Indians said 'How!' "

"I know how—just want chance!" he replied.

All teachings are concerned about how to do it, why to do it, for what purpose, for what goal. Zen simply gives you a chance, an opportunity, a certain context, a space in which you can become awakened. And that's exactly *my* work here: to create an opportunity, a space, a context, where you are *bound* to be awakened, where you *cannot* go on sleeping forever.

> *Dogo replied, "Since your arrival I have ever been giving you lessons on the matter of Zen discipline."*
> *"What kind of lesson could it have been?"*

Now Soshin is even more puzzled and bewildered because the Master says:

> *"Since your arrival I have ever been giving you lessons on the matter of Zen discipline."*

Strange are the ways of the real Masters. Indirect are their ways, subtle are their ways. Remember, he does not say "on Zen teaching"; he says "on Zen discipline —on the matter of Zen discipline."

"What kind of lesson could it have been?"

*"When you bring me a cup of tea in the morning,
I take it; when you serve me a meal, I accept it;
when you bow to me, I return it with a nod."*

The Master is saying, "Have you observed me?" That is
the essential core of Zen: watching, observing, being
aware. The Master is saying, "When you bring a cup of
tea in the morning for me, have you watched me—how
I take it, with what gratitude? Have you watched me—
how I accept it with great awareness? It is not just tea!"

Nothing is ordinary in the eyes of Zen; everything
is extraordinary because everything is divine. Zen
Masters have transformed ordinary things like tea-
drinking into religious ceremonies.

The tea ceremony is a great meditation; it takes
hours. In every Zen monastery there is a separate place
for the tea ceremony, a temple—a temple for tea! And
when people are invited by the Master they go to the
temple in absolute silence. The temple is surrounded
by rocks or a rock garden.

Sanantano has just now made a small rock garden
around my room, with a small waterfall. He has placed
the rocks in such a beautiful way—he seems to have
the insight, seems to have a communion with the
rocks. The rocks have come alive and they don't seem
to be just put any way, haphazardly; they seem to be in
a deep harmony.

Now, Sanantano is going to create many rock gar-
dens in the new commune so you can sit by those
rocks. . .and small bamboo huts for the tea ceremony.

And when a person goes—when the Master invites
someone for tea—he takes a bath, he meditates, he

cools himself down. He prepares himself because it is no ordinary occasion: an invitation from the Master. Then he walks the rocky path with full awareness, slowly. The closer he comes to the temple, the more alert he becomes. He becomes alert to the birds singing. He becomes alert to the flowers, their colors, their fragrance. And as he comes closer to the tearoom he starts hearing the noise of the samovar. He goes in. The shoes have to be left outside. He enters very silently, bows down to the Master, sits quietly in a corner listening to the samovar, the humming sound of the samovar . . . and the subtle fragrance of tea filling the room. It is a prayerful moment.

Then cups and saucers are given. The Master himself gives those cups and saucers . . . the way he gives. He pours the tea . . . the way he pours. Then they all sip the tea silently. It has to be sipped with tremendous awareness; then it becomes a meditation.

And if tea-drinking can become a meditation, then anything can become a meditation—cooking or washing your clothes, any activity can be transformed into meditation. And the real sannyasin, the real seeker, will transform all his acts into meditation. Only then, when meditation spreads over all your life, not only when you are awake in the day—slowly slowly it starts penetrating and permeating your being in sleep too—when it becomes just part of you, like breathing, like your heartbeat, then, only, have you attained to the discipline, to the essential discipline of Zen.

The Master said:

> *"When you bring me a cup of tea in the morning. . .*

"Have you observed or not? Are you asleep or awake? Can't you see the way I take it? *When you serve me a meal* . . . can't you see the way I accept it, with great gratitude, as if you have brought a treasure?

"*. . . when you bow to me, I return it with a nod.*

"Have I ever missed? Has it ever been noticed by you that I have not responded immediately? If you have been watching, then this is the real matter of Zen discipline. Do the same, do likewise!

"*How else do you expect to be taught in the discipline of Zen?*"

But you don't watch, you don't see. You go on rushing, doing things somehow, mechanically. And you go on falling into pitfalls, the *same* pitfalls again and again.

A nigger walks into a white bar with three friends, goes up to the barman and bets him $25 he can lick his own eye.

The barman thinks, "God-damned stupid nigger, nobody can lick his own eye," so he bets him the $25. The nigger takes out his glass eye and licks it and then bets the barman another $25 he can bite his other eye.

The barman thinks, "Oh boy, is this nigger ever dumb! Nobody could come in here with two glass eyes," and takes him up on the bet. The nigger takes his false teeth out and bites the other eye and the barman turns red with anger: "Smartass nigger!"

Then the nigger says, "I will bet you another $25. . . ."

"Wait a minute," says the barman. "No way. You think I'm stupid?"

"Oh, come on," says the nigger. I'll bet you double or nothing I can piss in that shot glass on the table on the other side of the room."

The barman stops, ponders a while and says, "Okay, even a stupid god-damned nigger couldn't do that! You're on. I'll bet you double or nothing!"

The nigger proceeds to piss all over the bar, the floor, everywhere. The barman starts laughing like hell, and wiping it up, says, "Boy, nigger, you are really dumb to think you could piss that far!"

And the nigger replies, "I'm not so dumb—see those three dudes over there? I bet them $300 I could piss all over the bar and you would wipe it up laughing!"

Man goes on doing the same; maybe a slightly different situation, but nothing very different. If you are asleep, if you are unconscious, you cannot watch, you cannot observe that again another pitfall . . . that again you are going into another mistake, another error, that you are again stumbling. Maybe it is a little bit different, because in life nothing is ever the same, but thousands of times you fall and still you don't learn the single thing worth learning. You learn all kinds of things in life except the one thing which can transform you, and that is the art of awareness.

Soshin hung his head for a while, pondering the puzzling words of the Master.
The Master said, "If you want to see, see right at once. When you begin to think, you miss the point."

These are tremendously significant words:

"If you want to see, see right at once. When you begin to think, you miss the point."

BECAUSE THINKING IS ONLY A WAY OF MISSING the point. When you hear the truth, *see* it immediately. Don't say, "I will think it over." Don't take notes saying, "Back home I will ponder over it." You are missing the whole point! Truth has an immediacy, and you are postponing it by thinking. And what can you think about truth? And whatsoever you think is going to be wrong. Truth is truth and untruth is untruth. You cannot make an untruth truth by thinking for years, and you cannot make a truth untruth by thinking for years. Nothing can be done about it; your thinking is absolutely irrelevant. *See* it. Seeing is relevant; thinking is not relevant.

That's why in the East we don't have any word to translate the English word "philosophy." We have a word, *darshan,* which is ordinarily used as a translation for philosophy but it is not right to do that. *Darshan* means seeing, and philosophy means thinking—and there is such a tremendous difference, such a vast difference, between the two. What greater difference can there be between two things—seeing and thinking?

Darshan simply means seeing. It is *not* thinking, it is awareness. Silently alert you sit by the side of the Master. He says something—or *shows* something rather —and you see it! If you are silent and aware you are bound to see it, you cannot miss it. If you hang your head and you start thinking, you have forgotten about the Master; you are lost in your own words. You are translating the Master into your own words—and you cannot translate those heights, those depths. And whatsoever you translate will be something utterly different from what the Master has said.

Three Frenchmen, while practicing their English, got around to discussing the wife of a friend who was childless.

"She is unbearable," said one.

"No, that is the wrong word. She is inconceivable."

"No, no, you are both wrong," said the third. "What you mean is she is impregnable."

Now, you can go on thinking. . . . When the Master speaks, he speaks from the heights of awareness—and you listen in the darkness of your valley. Don't translate and don't try to figure it out, what he is saying. Just listen.

Just the other day somebody asked: "Listening to you unquestioningly, accepting it, isn't it a way of being conditioned by you?"

Listening silently does not mean that you are agreeing with me. It is not a question of agreement or disagreement. Listening silently does not mean that you are accepting me or rejecting me. If you are accepting you are not silent; activity is there—the activity of accepting. If you are agreeing with me that means you are already translating me. If you are rejecting me that is negative activity; if you accept me that is positive activity. And to be silent simply means no activity at all. You are simply here . . . just being here, only available, no question of agreeing or disagreeing.

And the beauty of truth is that the moment you hear the truth something inside you responds, says yes. It is not agreement of the mind, remember; it comes from your totality. Every fiber of your being, every cell of your body, nods in tremendous joy, "Yes!" Not that you say yes—it is not said, it is not verbalized at all. It is silently there. And when you hear some untruth, in the same way there is a no; your whole being says "no." That is not mental either.

This is a totally different approach. The West has not been able to evolve it yet; the East has evolved it. For centuries we have been working on this subtle method, polishing it, polishing it. It has become a mirror.

The East knows how to just sit in silence, without agreeing or disagreeing, because we have discovered one fundamental thing: that truth is already inside you. If you hear the truth from the outside your truth will be awakened, it will be provoked. Suddenly you will say "Yes!"—as if you had known it already. It is a recognition, it is a remembrance. You are simply being reminded by the Master about that which you have forgotten. It is not a question of agreement or disagreement—no, not at all.

I am not interested in creating beliefs in you and I am not interested in giving you any kind of ideology. My whole effort here is—as it has always been of all the Buddhas since the beginnings of time—to provoke truth in you. I know it is already there; it just needs a synchronicity. It just needs something to trigger the process of recognition in you.

The Master speaks not to give you the truth, but to help you to recognize the truth that is already within you. The Master is only a mirror. You see your own original face in deep silence, sitting by his side.

The Master said, "If you want to see, see right at once. When you begin to think, you miss the point."

Try it
My Way

The first question

Bhagwan,
When I am working in the West I feel like an
orange warrior, and I like it. When I am here I
feel meditative, and I like it. Is the part of
myself that still needs to fight an obstacle to
becoming a good disciple?

Deva Majid,

ASANNYASIN HAS TO BE LIQUID, FLOWING. He has not to be stonelike, fixated. He has to be like flowing water so he can take any form. Whatsoever is the need of the moment he responds accordingly—not according to any fixed pattern, not according to any *a priori* idea of how a sannyasin should be. There is nothing like that in *my* vision of sannyas.

Never ask me how a sannyasin should be, because that will become a pattern and you will act out of the pattern. And any action out of a patterned life is wrong. One has to be loose, relaxed, so that one can respond to the situation. And situations go on changing. In the West it is different; here it is different.

So when it is needed to be a warrior, be a warrior; and when it is needed to be meditative, be meditative. When it is needed to be an extrovert, be an extrovert; and when it is needed to be an introvert, be an introvert. This fluidity is sannyas. If you become fixated, then you are no more alive—you have become obsessed. Then you are an extrovert or an introvert, worldly or other-worldly, but you are no more my sannyasin.

My sannyasin is indescribable, as indescribable as God himself, as life itself, as love itself—as inexpressible as existence itself. A sannyasin is in total harmony with existence, so whatsoever the need of the moment, the sannyasin goes with the moment, flows with the river. He does not go upstream; he does not have any idea of how things should be. He has no "ought"; he has no commandments in his mind to be fulfilled, to be followed.

This is true discipline: discipline that brings freedom, discipline that liberates.

The second question

Bhagwan,
I cannot drop the habit of chain-smoking.
I have tried hard but I have failed always.
Is it a sin to smoke?

Gurucharan,

DON'T MAKE A MOUNTAIN OUT OF A MOLEHILL! Religious people are very skillful in doing that. Now, what are you really doing when you are smoking? Just taking some smoke inside your lungs and letting it out. It is a kind of *pranayama*—filthy, dirty, but still a *pranayama!* You are doing yoga, in a stupid way. It is not sin. It may be foolish but it is not a sin, certainly.

There is only one sin and that is unawareness, and only one virtue and that is awareness.

Do whatsoever you are doing, but remain a witness to it, and immediately the quality of your doing is transformed. I will not tell you not to smoke; that you have tried. You must have been told by many so-called saints not to smoke: "Because if you smoke you will fall into hell." God is not so stupid as your saints are. Throwing somebody into hell just because he was smoking cigarettes will be absolutely unnecessary.

One morning, Weintraub went to a restaurant and ordered bacon with his eggs. He was an orthodox Jew and his wife kept a strictly kosher home, but Weintraub felt the need just this once.

As Weintraub was about to leave the restaurant, he stopped in the door frozen with terror. The sky was filled with black clouds, there was lightning, and the ground shook with the rumble of thunder.

"Can you imagine!" he exclaimed. "All that fuss over a little piece of bacon!"

But that's what your so-called saints have been telling you down the ages, for centuries.

Smoking is unhealthy, unhygienic, but not a sin. It becomes a sin only if you are doing it unconsciously— it is not smoking that makes it a sin but unconsciousness.

Let me emphasize the fact. You can do your prayer every day unconsciously; then your prayer is a sin. You can become addicted to your prayer. If you miss the prayer one day, the whole day you will feel something is wrong, something is missing, some gap. It is the same with smoking or with drinking; there is no difference in it. Your prayer has become a mechanical habit; it has become a master over you. It bosses you; you are just a servant, a slave to it. If you don't do it, it forces you to do it.

So it is not a question of smoking. You may be doing your Transcendental Meditation every day regularly, and it may be just the same. If the quality of uncon-sciousness is there, if mechanicalness is there, if it has become a fixed routine, if it has become a habit and you are a victim of the habit and you cannot put it aside, you are no more a master of yourself, then it is a sin. But its being a sin comes out of your unconscious-ness, not out of the act itself.

No act is virtuous, no act is a sin. What consciousness is behind the act—everything depends on that.

You say: *I cannot drop the habit of chain-smoking.*

I am less interested in your chain-smoking; I am more interested in your habit. *Any* habit that becomes a force, a dominating force over you, is a sin. One should live more in freedom. One should be able to do things not according to habits but according to the situations.

Life is continuously changing—it is a flux—and habits are stagnant. The more you are surrounded by habits, the more you are closed to life. You are not open, you don't have windows. You don't have any communication with life; you go on repeating your habits. They don't fit; they are not the right response to the situation, to the moment. They are always lagging behind, they are always falling short. That's the failure of your life.

So remember: I am against all kinds of habits. Good or bad is not the point; there is no good habit as such, there is no bad habit as such. Habits are all bad because habit means something unconscious has become a dominating factor in your life, has become decisive. You are no more the deciding factor. The response is not coming out of awareness but out of a pattern, structure, that you have learned in the past.

Two members of the Shalom Retirement Home, Blustein and Levin, were strolling past the home of Nelson Rockefeller.

"If I only had that man's millions," sighed Blustein, "I would be richer than he is."

"Don't be a dummy," said Levin. "If you had his millions you would be as rich as he is, not any richer."

"You are wrong," said Blustein, "don't forget—I could give Hebrew lessons on the side!"

That's what he has been doing. Even if he becomes Nelson Rockefeller he will go on giving Hebrew lessons on the side. That's how people are living, just according to habits.

I have seen many rich people living very poor lives. Before they became rich their habits became settled— and their habits became settled when they were poor. That's why you find so much miserliness in rich people; it comes from the habits that became ingrained in them when they were poor.

One of the richest men in the world—not *one* of the richest but *the* richest man in the world it is thought— was the Nizam of Hyderabad. His collection of dia-

monds was the greatest in the world because he owned
the diamond mines of Golconda which have provided
the greatest diamonds to the world. The Kohinoor
comes from Golconda. It was once in the Nizam's
possession. He had so many diamonds that it is said
that no one has ever been able to calculate exactly the
price of his collection. Thousands and thousands of
diamonds—they were not counted, they were
weighed!

But he was one of the most miserly men in the
world. He used a single cap for thirty years. It was
stinking but he wouldn't change it. He continued to
wear the same coat for almost his whole life and he
would not give it to be washed because they might
destroy it. He was so miserly—you cannot imagine—
that he would collect half-smoked cigarettes from the
guests' ashtrays and then smoke them. The richest man
in the world smoking cigarette butts smoked by others!
The first thing he would do whenever a guest left was
to search in the ashtrays and collect the ends of the
cigarettes.

When he died, his greatest diamond was found in his
dirty shoes. He was hiding it in his shoe! Maybe he had
some idea behind it—that maybe he would be able to
take it with him to the other world. Maybe he was
afraid: "When I am dead, people may steal it." It was
the greatest diamond; he used that diamond as a paper-
weight on his table. Before he died he must have put it
inside his shoe.

Even when one is dying one is moving in old habits,
following old patterns.

I have heard:

The old Mulla Nasruddin had become a very rich

man. When he felt death approaching he decided to make some arrangements for his funeral, so he ordered a beautiful coffin made of ebony wood with satin pillows inside. He also had a beautiful silk kaftan made for his dead body to be dressed in.

The day the tailor delivered the kaftan, Mulla Nasruddin tried it on to see how it would look, but suddenly he exclaimed, "What is this! Where are the pockets?"

Gurucharan, smoking or no smoking, that is not important. Maybe if you continue to smoke you will die a little earlier. So what? The world is so overpopulated, you will do some good by dying a little earlier. Maybe you will have tuberculosis. So what? Tuberculosis is now almost like the common cold. In fact, there is no cure for the common cold but there is a cure for tuberculosis. I know it because I suffer from a common cold. To have tuberculosis is to be very fortunate.

A man was suffering from a common cold for many years. All the doctors were tired of the man because nobody was able to cure him. Then a new doctor came to the town. All the other doctors told the new doctor, "Beware of this man! He is going to haunt you! He is a nuisance—his cold cannot be cured."

In fact, there is no cure for the common cold. They say that if you take medicine it goes within seven days; if you don't take the medicine it goes in one week.

So the new doctor was ready and the man appeared, as predicted by the others. The new doctor said, "I can cure it. You do one thing"—it must have been wintertime, just like this morning—he told him, "You do one thing: tomorrow, early in the morning, before sunrise, go to the lake; swim in the lake naked, then stand on the bank in the cold wind."

The man said, "Are you mad or something? How is that going to cure my common cold?"

The doctor said, "Who told you that it is going to cure your common cold? It will give you influenza, and I can cure that!"

So it is possible, Gurucharan, that you may die two years earlier, you may get tuberculosis—but it is not a sin. Don't be worried about *that*.

If you really want to do something about your life, dropping smoking is not going to help—because I know people who drop smoking; then they start chewing gum. The same old stupidity! Or if they are Indians they start chewing pan; it is the same. You will do something or other. Your unconsciousness will demand some activity, some occupation. It is an occupation. And it is only a symptom; it is not really the problem. It is not the root of the problem.

Have you not observed? Whenever you feel emotionally disturbed you immediately start smoking. It gives you a kind of relief; you become occupied. Your mind is distracted from the emotional problem. Whenever people feel tense they start smoking. The problem is tension, the problem is emotional disturbance—the problem is somewhere else; smoking is just an occupation. So you become engaged in taking the smoke in and out and you forget for the time being . . . because mind cannot think of two things together, remember it. One of the fundamentals of mind is: it can think only of one thing at one time; it is one-dimensional. So if you are smoking and thinking of smoking, then from *all* other anxieties you are distracted.

That's the whole secret of the so-called spiritual mantras: they are nothing but distractions, like smoking. You repeat "Om, Om, Om," or "Ram, Ram, Ram," or "Allah, Allah, Allah"—that is just giving mind an occupation. And all these people who teach mantras say, "Repeat it as quickly as possible, so that between two repetitions there is not even a small gap. Let them overlap—so 'Ram Ram Ram'—don't leave a gap between two Rams, otherwise some thought may enter. Repeat like crazy!"

Yes, it will give you a certain relief—the same relief that comes from smoking, because your mind will be distracted from the anxieties and the world. You will forget about the world; you have created a trick. All mantras are tricks, but they are spiritual. Chain-smoking is also a mantra. It is a worldly mantra; non-religious you can call it, secular.

The real problem is the habit.

You say: *I have tried hard to drop it. . . .*

You have not tried to be conscious of it; without trying to be conscious you have tried to drop it. It is not possible. It will come back, because your mind is the same; its needs are the same, its problems are the same, its anxieties, tensions are the same, its anguish is the same. And when those anxieties arise, what will you do? Immediately, mechanically, you will start searching for the cigarettes.

You may have decided again and again, and again and again you have failed—not because smoking is such a great phenomenon that you cannot get out of it, but because you are trying from the wrong end. Rather than becoming aware of the whole situation—why you smoke in the first place—rather than becoming aware of the process of smoking, you are simply trying to drop it. It is like pruning the leaves of a tree without cutting the roots.

And my whole concern here is to cut the roots, not to prune the tree. By pruning the leaves and the branches the tree will become thicker, the foliage will become thicker. You will not destroy the tree; you will be helping it, in fact. If you really want to get out of it you will have to look deeper, not into the symptoms but the roots. Where are the roots?

You must be a deeply anxiety-ridden person, otherwise chain-smoking is not possible; chain-smoking is a by-product. You must be so concerned about a thousand and one disturbances inside, you must be carrying such a big load of worries on your heart, on your chest, that you don't even know how to forget them. You don't know how to drop them—smoking at least helps you to forget about them.

You say: *I have tried hard. . . .*

Now one thing has to be understood. The hypnotists have discovered a fundamental law; they call it the Law of Reverse Effect. If you try hard to do something without understanding the fundamentals, just the opposite will be the result.

It is like when you are learning how to ride on a bicycle. You are on a silent road, no traffic, early in the morning, and you see a red milestone just standing there by the side of the road like Hanuman. A sixty-foot-wide road and just a small milestone, and you become afraid: you may get to the milestone, you may hit against the milestone. Now you forget about the sixty-foot-wide road. In fact, even if you go blindfolded there is not much chance of your encountering the milestone, crashing into the milestone, but with open eyes now the whole road is forgotten; you have become focussed. In the first place, that redness is very focussing. And you are so much afraid!—you want to avoid it. You have forgotten that you are on a bicycle; you have forgotten everything. Now the only problem for you is how to avoid this stone; otherwise you may harm yourself, you may crash into it.

Now the crash is absolutely inevitable; you are bound to crash with the stone. And then you will be surprised: "I tried hard." In fact it is *because* you tried hard that you reached the stone. And the closer you come, the harder you try to avoid it; but the harder you try to avoid it, the more focussed you become on it. It becomes a hypnotic force, it hypnotizes you. It becomes like a magnet.

It is a very fundamental law in life. Many people try avoiding many things and they fall into the same things. Try to avoid anything with great effort and you are bound to fall into the same pit. You cannot avoid it; that is not the way to avoid it.

Be relaxed. Don't try hard, because it is through relaxation that you can become aware, not by trying hard. Be calm, quiet, silent.

I will suggest: smoke as much as you want to smoke. It is not a sin in the first place. I give you the guarantee—I will be responsible. I take the sin on myself, so if you meet God on Judgment Day you can just tell him that this fellow is responsible. And I will stand there as a witness for you that you are not responsible. So don't be worried about its being a sin. Relax and don't try to drop it with effort. No, that is not going to help.

Zen believes in effortless understanding.

So this is my suggestion: smoke as much as you want

to smoke—just smoke meditatively. If Zen people can drink tea meditatively, why can't you smoke meditatively? In fact, tea contains the same stimulant as the cigarettes contain; it is the same stimulant, there is not much difference. Smoke meditatively, very religiously. Make it a ceremony. Try it *my* way.

Make a small corner in your house just for smoking; a small temple devoted, dedicated to the god of smoking. First bow down to your cigarette packet. Have a little chit-chat, talk to the cigarettes. Enquire, "How are you?" And then very slowly take a cigarette out—very slowly, as slowly as you can, because only if you take it very slowly will you be aware. Don't do it in a mechanical way, as you always do. Then tap the cigarette on the packet very slowly and for as long as you want. There is no hurry either. Then take the lighter, bow down to the lighter. These are great gods, deities! Light is God, so why not the lighter?

Then start smoking very slowly, just like *vipassana*. Don't do it like a *pranayama*—quick and fast and deep —but very slowly. Buddha says: Breathe naturally. So you smoke naturally: very slow, no hurry. If it is a sin you are in a hurry. If it is a sin you want to finish it as soon as possible. If it is a sin you don't want to look at it. You go on reading the newspaper and you go on smoking. Who wants to look at a sin? But it is not a sin, so watch it—watch each of your acts.

Divide your acts into small fragments so you can move very slowly. And you will be surprised: by watching your smoking, slowly slowly smoking will become less and less. And one day suddenly . . . it is gone. You have not made any effort to drop it; it has dropped of its own accord, because by becoming aware of a dead pattern, a routine, a mechanical habit, you have created, you have released, a new energy of consciousness in you. Only that energy can help you; nothing else will ever help.

And it is not only so with smoking, Gurucharan, it is so with everything else in life: don't try too hard to change yourself. That leaves scars. Even if you change, your change will remain superficial. And you will find a substitute somewhere; you will *have* to find a substitute, otherwise you will feel empty.

And when something withers away of its own accord because you have become so silently aware of the stupidity of it that no effort is needed, when it simply falls, just like a dead leaf falling from a tree, it leaves no scar behind and it leaves no ego behind.

If you drop something by effort, it creates great ego. You start thinking, "Now I am a very virtuous man because I don't smoke." If you think that smoking is a sin, naturally, obviously, if you drop it you will think you are a very virtuous man.

That's how your virtuous men are. Somebody does not smoke, somebody does not drink, somebody eats only once a day, somebody does not eat in the night, somebody has even stopped drinking water in the night . . . and they are all great saints! These are saintly qualities, great virtues!

We have made religion so silly. It has lost all glory. It has become as stupid as people are. But the whole thing depends on your attitude: if you think something is a sin, then your virtue will be just the opposite of it.

I emphasize: not-smoking is not virtue, smoking is not sin; awareness is virtue, unawareness is sin. And then the same law is applicable to your whole life.

The third question

Bhagwan,
The other day in discourse you said that
sannyas only comes when the point of suicide
has been reached. But I did not feel suicidal
when I took sannyas, only in deep love with
you. My life seemed rich, but you have made it
infinitely richer. Am I not a true sannyasin
because I don't feel suicidal?

Prem Sunderam,

AND WHAT IS LOVE? It is the greatest suicide in the world! Love means committing suicide: the suicide of the ego. Love means dropping the ego. That's why people are so much afraid of love. They talk about it, they pretend also. They manage to befool others and themselves too that they love. But they avoid love—because love requires you first to die; only then are you resurrected.

So what I said is absolutely true and absolutely applicable to you. And life certainly becomes richer. The more you die to the ego, the richer your life is, the more your life is full of overflowing love and joy and ecstasy.

No, you are my true sannyasin—but love is the ultimate in suicide. All other suicides are small suicides. Somebody commits suicide; that is only physical. Love is psychological suicide and meditation is spiritual suicide. In love you die psychologically, you drop the psychological ego, and in meditation you drop the very idea of the self, even of the supreme self. You become a nothingness . . . and in that nothingness blooms the white lotus of a Buddha.

The fourth question

Bhagwan,
How can I learn the secrets of life?

Rabindra,

THERE ARE NO SECRETS IN LIFE. Or you can say: life is an open secret. Everything is available, nothing is hidden. All that you need is just eyes to see.

It is like a blind man asking: "I want to learn the secret of light." All that he needs is treatment of the eyes so that he can see. Light is available, it is not a secret. But he is blind—for him there is no light. What to say about light? For him there is not even darkness— because even to see darkness eyes are needed. A blind man cannot see darkness. If you can see darkness you can see light; they are two aspects of the same coin. The blind man knows nothing of darkness and nothing of light. Now he wants to learn the secrets of light.

We can only help him, not by teaching him great truths about light—they will be useless—but by operating on his eyes.

That's exactly what is being done here. This is an operation theater. The moment you become a sann-yasin you are getting ready for the operation table, and you have to pass through many surgical operations. That's what all the therapies are. And if you survive all the therapies, then I am there finally to finish you off!

The moment the ego disappears, all the secrets are open secrets. Life is not like a fist; it is an open hand.

But people enjoy the idea that life has secrets—hidden secrets. Just to avoid their blindness they have created the idea of hidden secrets, of esoteric knowledge which is not available to anybody, or is available only to great adepts who live in Tibet or in the Himalayas, or who are no more in their bodies, who live only in astral bodies and appear only to a few chosen people. And all kinds of nonsense has been perpetuated down the ages for the simple reason that you want to avoid seeing, recognizing the simple fact of your blindness. Rather than saying, "I am blind," you say, "Life's secrets are very hidden; they are not easily available. You will need great initiation."

Life is not esoteric at all. It is written on each leaf of each tree, on each pebble on the seashore; it is contained in each ray of the sun—whatever you come across is life in all its beauty. And life is not afraid of you, so why should it hide itself? In fact, *you* are hiding, continuously trying to hide yourself. You are closing yourself against life because you are afraid of life. You are afraid to live—because life requires a constant death.

One has to die every moment to the past. That is a great requirement of life—simple if you understand that the past is no more. Slip out of it, snap out of it! It is finished. Close the chapter, don't go on carrying it! And then life is available to you.

But you remain in the past; the past goes on hanging around you, the hangover never ends. And rather than coming to the present, the hangover of the past pushes you towards the future. So either you are in the memories or you are in your imagination. These are the two ways to miss life; otherwise there is no need to miss life. Just drop out of memories and out of imagination. Past is no more, future is not yet; both are non-existential. All that exists is the present, the now. Now is God.

Enter the doors of the now and all is revealed—instantly revealed, immediately revealed. Life is not a miser: it never hides anything, it does not hold anything back. It is ready to give all, totally and unconditionally. But *you* are not ready.

And Rabindra, you ask: *How can I learn the secrets of life?*

It is not a question of learning; it is more a question of unlearning. You have already learned too much: the Vedas, the Upanishads, the Gita, the Koran, the Bible, the Talmud. Thousands of scriptures are there inside you, clamoring, making noise, fighting with each other; all kinds of ideologies constantly trying to attract your attention. Your mind is a mess! It is overcrowded, it is a multitude. Unlearn! All that you have accumulated up to now as knowledge, unlearn it.

Zen people are right when they say: *Not knowing is the most intimate.*

Unlearning is the process that can bring you to that beautiful space of not knowing. And then observe. Observe life without any knowledge interpreting it. You have become so accustomed to interpretation.

The moment you see the sunset, immediately, habitually, you repeat words that you have heard from others: "What a beautiful sunset!" You don't mean anything by it; you are not even looking at the sunset. You have not allowed it to penetrate to your heart. You are not feeling any wonder. You are not in a state of awe. You have not fallen on your knees. You are not looking with unblinking eyes, absorbing. Nothing of that. Just a casual remark: "What a beautiful sunset!" Just a way of speaking, a mannerism, showing that you are cultured, sophisticated, that you know what beauty is, that you have a great aesthetic sense, that you have great sensitivity towards nature. You are not looking at the sunset. Have you ever looked at the sunset? If you had looked you would not have asked this question; the sunset would have told you all.

Have you ever looked at a roseflower? Yes, you say, "It is beautiful!" You may repeat the famous saying: "A rose is a rose is a rose," but you are not seeing the rose. You are full of words, all kinds of jargon—poetic, philosophic—but between you and the roseflower there is such a wall, a China Wall. Behind that wall you are hiding.

And you are asking: *How can I learn the secrets of life?*

And life goes on utterly nude, utterly naked, absolutely available. All that is required is a not-knowing state, an empty space which can absorb it, which can receive it. Only when you are in a state of not knowing are you a host, and then life becomes a guest.

Just observe with no evaluation. Don't say "good," don't say "bad"; don't say "beautiful," don't say "ugly." Don't say anything at all! Without saying anything, without bringing your mind in, just watch with utterly empty eyes, like a mirror. Reflect the moon, the stars, the sun, the trees, the people, the animals, the birds. And life will pour itself into your being. And it is an inexhaustible source of energy. And energy is delight.

William Blake is right when he says: Energy is delight. And when life pours its energy into your being it rejuvenates you, it revitalizes you; you are constantly reborn. A real, alive person is born again and again every *moment.* He is fresh, he is always young. Even when he dies he is fresh and young. Even in the moment of death, life is pouring more and more energy into him. His way of approaching life—without mind—helps him to see not only life but death too. And when you are able to see life, you are able to see death. And to see death means there is no death; all is life, and eternal, beginningless, endless. And you are part of this infinite celebration.

Just watch, be alert, and function from a state of innocence. Your question seems to be knowledgeable.

You say: *How can I learn the secrets of life?*

You are still asking like a student, a schoolboy.

Life is ready every moment to embrace you. *You* are hiding away from life because you are afraid. You want life on your terms. You want life to be Hindu or Mohammedan or Christian, and life cannot do that. You want life according to the Gita or the Koran, and life cannot do that.

Don't put conditions on life. Putting conditions on life is ugly, violent, stupid. Remain unconditionally open. . .and suddenly some bells in your heart start ringing, in tune with the whole. A music arises, a melody is born. You are no more separate as a learner, as a knower. Finally you are not even separate as an observer; the observer and the observed become one ultimately.

That is the moment of enlightenment, of Buddhahood, when you are part of this whole, an intrinsic part, inseparable. Then you *are* life—what is the need to learn anything? You *are* it; you are not separate from it. Who is going to learn and about what? You are life. Then experiencing arises: not knowing but experiencing, not knowledge but wisdom.

Raul was sitting against the wall of his friend Pablo's adobe shack. Pablo came out of the house with a butterfly in his hand.

"Ay, Pablo," called Raul. "Where are you going with the butterfly?"

"I am going to get some butter," replied Pablo.

"Oh, you foolish fellow!" said Raul. "You cannot get butter with a butterfly!"

A few minutes later, to Raul's astonishment, Pablo returned with a bucket of butter.

In a little while Pablo came out, this time carrying a jar of horseflies.

"Ay, Pablo," called Raul, "where are you going with them horseflies?"

"Where you think?" answered Pablo. "To get horses, of course!"

Pablo returned in a few minutes leading a pair of beautiful stallions.

"See, I told you!" said Pablo to the amazed Raul.

Ten minutes later Pablo came out clutching a handful of pussy willows.

"Ay, Pablo!" shouted Raul. "Wait for me—I go with you!"

Just observe. Nothing is hidden—just observe. And slowly slowly you will start going with life. Slowly slowly you will not remain separate, you will follow life. And to follow life is to be religious. Not to follow

Christ, not to follow Buddha, but to follow life is to be religious.

The fifth question

Bhagwan,
I can find the answer to all the questions I ask
you within myself, but still I would like to ask
you one—just for fun, simply taking up your
invitation. Is it really possible for an ordinary
person like myself to live in this world, earning
and spending, and still be in the state of
no-mind constantly?

Deva David,

I WILL NOT ANSWER THIS QUESTION—just for fun! If you can find the answer to all the questions, find out the answer to this one too!

And you don't seem to be an *ordinary* person—one who can find all the answers to all the questions within himself can't be an ordinary person, otherwise how will you define the extraordinary?

No, I will not bother you with an answer—you find it within yourself. When you cannot find it, then ask me again.

The sixth question

Bhagwan,
Can't one believe in God without seeing him?

Surendra Mohan,

WHO IS TELLING YOU TO BELIEVE IN GOD? I am against all belief. You must be a very new comer here. Belief is irreligious, as much as disbelief is. Belief means you don't know yet you have accepted something. It is cowardly—you have not enquired. You are pretending, you are a hypocrite.

All believers are hypocrites—Catholic and communist, Jainas and Jews—all. Believers are hypocrites. They don't know and yet they pretend *as if* they know. What is belief? It is playing the game of "as if." And the same is true about disbelief.

The communist knows *not* that there is no God, just as the Hindu knows not that there is a God. The Hindu believes there is a God, the communist believes there is no God. Disbelief is also a kind of belief—a negative kind of belief. And that's why it is so easy to become a Hindu from being a communist or a communist from being a Hindu.

It is a well-known fact that before the Russian revolution Russia was one of the *most* religious countries in the world. Then what happened? After ten years of revolution, the whole country became atheistic. The same people who were fanatical believers became fanatical *dis*believers! On the surface it looks puzzling, but it is not. The fanaticism is the same; nothing has changed. They were fanatic Christians, now they are fanatic comm   . They believed madly, now they disbelieve mad , their madness is the same. And their belief was wrong because they had not experienced it, and their disbelief is wrong because they have not yet experienced the *absence* of God.

Surendra Mohan, you ask me: *Can't one believe
in God without seeing him?*

In the first place there is no need to believe in God.
And if you believe you will never be able to know him.
Belief will become a barrier; belief is always a barrier.
Belief means you are carrying a prejudice, and you will
not be able to see that which is. You will project your
own idea.

That's why a Hindu, when he comes to a vision of
God, will see Krishna with the flute. He will never see
Christ, he will never see Mahavira, he will never see
Buddha. And the Christian? He has never seen Krishna
or Buddha. And a Jew? He has his own ideas. So when
you see, what you see is not really the real but your
own projection, your own idea.

Remember: as long as you have even a single idea inside you, your experience is going to be distorted by it.

My suggestion to *my* people is: don't carry any idea
of God, for or against. Don't carry any image of God.
In fact, God is absolutely irrelevant—be meditative!
And meditation means: drop all thoughts, drop all ideologies, drop all knowledge. Drop the mind itself.

And then when you are in a state of no-mind, something unimaginable, unbelievable, unpredictable, inexpressible, is experienced. You can call it God, you can
call it truth, you can call it *nirvana,* or whatsoever you
want to call it. You are free because no word describes
it, hence any word is as good as any other. But don't
carry any belief.

And what do you mean: ". . . without seeing him"?
Do you think someday you will see God? Is God a person? That's how people think: God is like Rama, always
carrying a bow with arrows. Now, in the twentieth cen-

tury, carrying a bow would look so foolish. Give him
an atom bomb—that will look far more contemporary!
Jesus on the cross . . . twenty centuries have passed.
Now we have electric chairs! Give him an electric chair.
At least he can rest on the chair! Still you go on giving
him a cross. Make your ideas a little more contemporary. They are all out of date.

What do you mean by *"seeing God"*? Is he a person?
Will you say hello and will you shake hands with him?
God is not a person, hence God cannot be seen in that
sense. God is a presence.

There is no God but godliness. It is a quality, a fragrance. You experience it, you don't see it. And when
you experience it, it is not something out there as an
object; it is something *in here,* in the heart of your
hearts. It is your subjectivity, it is your consciousness.

So there is no question of belief and there is no question of seeing either.

But people are brought up in all kinds of beliefs and
they go on seeing through their prejudices. So anything
that fits with their prejudices enters inside; anything
that does not fit with their prejudice is prevented from
entering.

An elephant escaped from the local zoo and made his
way into the vegetable garden of one of the town's
most prominent matrons. Unfortunately this lady had
only just returned from a cocktail party where she had
had just a little too much to drink. She was not too
drunk, however, to see the beast in her garden, and she
had the presence of mind to call the police.

"Quick," she said, "there is some kind of huge,
strange looking animal in my garden."

"What is he doing?" asked the desk sergeant.

"He seems to be picking lettuce with his tail!"

"Oh, really?" replied the wary policeman. "And what is he doing with it?"

The lady peered out into her garden once more and then said, "Sergeant, even if I told you, you would never believe it!"

God has been experienced. Nobody has ever been able to say exactly what that experience is. And even if somebody tries to say it, you are not going to believe it. Your prejudices, your *a priori* ideas, will prevent you.

No, Surendra Mohan, no need to believe in God; no need even to believe that one day you are going to see him. In fact, God is not a religious subject at all—you will be surprised when you hear it—God is a philosophic subject. It is for those useless people who go on endlessly into logic-chopping and hair-splitting. It is for those people to discuss God.

A religious person is not interested in God; he is more interested in the very source of his being, who he is: "Who am I?" That is the *most* fundamental religious question—not God, not heaven, not hell, but "Who am I?" And if you can find the truth of your own being you will have found all the truth that is necessary to know and is worth knowing. You will have found God and you will have found *nirvana* and you will have found all that the seers, the *rishis,* the Buddhas, the prophets, down the ages, have been telling you to enquire into.

But don't make a philosophical enquiry, otherwise you will end up with a conclusion. And all conclusions are dangerous because once you conclude you become fanatical about your conclusion, you start clinging to it. You become afraid of truth—because who knows?

truth may disturb your conclusion, and your conclusion is so cozy and so convenient, and it has helped to
give you a certain feeling of security. So you go on
clinging to your conclusion—and your conclusion is
your conclusion.

If you are unaware, what value can your conclusion
have? Your conclusion cannot be bigger than you,
your conclusion cannot be higher than you. Your conclusion will be as high, as deep, as you are high and you
are deep. Your conclusion will only reflect you.

God is not a conclusion. It is not arrived at by logical
processes—by believing, by discussing, by analyzing,
no. All mind processes have to cease. When all processes have ceased, something—call it XYZ—suddenly
wells up within you. A few qualities can be indicated:
you will feel tremendously ecstatic, blissful, at home, at
ease. For the first time existence will be your home.
You will not be an outsider, a stranger. For the first
time there will be no conflict between you and existence, no struggle for the survival of the fittest. For the
first time you will be in a state of let-go. And in let-go
wells up great joy.

You will be able to sing the song that you have
brought in your heart and is still unsung. You will be
able to bloom into thousands of flowers. Or as in the
East we say: you will bloom into a thousand-petalled
lotus of consciousness, of awareness. That is God—or
better, godliness.

The seventh question

Bhagwan,
I know you are against marriage, but I still
want to get married. Can I have your
blessings?

Rakesh,

MEDITATE OVER MURPHY'S MAXIM: A fool and his cool are soon parted.

It is not yet published anywhere, but Asha is the custodian of Murphy's unpublished manuscripts, so she goes on supplying these maxims of Murphy to me. Meditate over it: A fool and his cool are soon parted.

That's what marriage is going to be. Only fools think in terms of legality; otherwise, love is enough. And I am not against marriage—I am for love. If love becomes your marriage, good; but don't hope that marriage can bring love. That is not possible. Love can become a marriage. You have to work very consciously to transform your love into a marriage.

Ordinarily, people destroy their love. They do *everything* to destroy it and then they suffer. And they go on saying, "What went wrong?" They destroy—they do everything to destroy it.

There is a tremendous desire and longing for love, but love needs great awareness. Only then can it reach its highest climax—and that highest climax *is* marriage. It has nothing to do with law. It is a merging of two hearts into totality. It is the functioning of two persons in synchronicity—that is marriage.

But people try love and because they are unconscious . . . their longing is good, but their love is full of jealousy, full of possessiveness, full of anger, full of nastiness. Soon they destroy it. Hence for centuries they have depended on marriage. Better to start by marriage so that the law can protect you from destroying it. The society, the government, the court, the policeman, the priest, they will all force you to live in the institution of marriage, and you will be just a slave. If marriage is an institution, you are going to be a slave in it. Only slaves want to live in institutions.

Marriage is a totally different phenomenon: it is the climax of love. Then it is good. I am not against marriage—I am for the *real* marriage. I am against the false, the pseudo, that exists. But it is an arrangement. It gives you a certain security, safety, occupation. It keeps you engaged. Otherwise, it gives you no enrichment, it gives you no nourishment.

So, Rakesh, if you want to get married according to me, only then can I give you my blessings.

Learn to love, and drop all that goes against love. It is an uphill task. It is the greatest art in existence, to be able to love. One needs such refinement, such inner culture, such meditativeness, so that one can see immediately how one goes on destroying. If you can avoid being destructive, if you become creative in your relationship; if you support it, nourish it; if you are capable of compassion for the other person, not only passion. . . . Passion alone is not able to sustain love; compassion is needed. If you are able to be compassionate towards the other; if you are able to accept his limitations, his imperfections; if you are able to accept him the way he is or she is and *still* love—then one day a marriage happens. That may take years. That may take your whole life.

You can have my blessings, but for a legal marriage

you need not have my blessings—and my blessings won't be of any help either. And beware! Before you jump into it, give it a second thought.

A woman walks into a pet shop and sees a bird with a big beak. "What is that strange looking bird?" she asks the proprietor.

"That is a gobble bird," he answers.

"Why do you call him a gobble bird?"

The man says to the bird, "Gobble bird, my chair!"

The bird immediately starts pecking away and gobbles up the chair.

"I will buy him," the woman says.

The owner asks why.

"Well," she says, "when my husband comes home he will see the bird and ask, 'What is that?' I will say, 'A gobble bird.' And then he will say, 'Gobble bird, my foot!' "

Just be a little aware before you move! My blessings won't help. Marriage is a trap and your wife sooner or later will find a gobble bird.

Mrs. Moskowitz loved chicken soup. One evening she was spooning it up when three of her husband's friends came in. "Mrs. Moskowitz," the spokesman said, "we are here to tell you that your husband, Izzy, has been killed in an automobile accident."

Mrs. Moskowitz continued eating her soup. Again they told her. Still no reaction.

"Look," said the puzzled speaker, "we are telling you that your husband is dead!"

She went right on with the soup. "Gentlemen," she said between mouthfuls, "soon as I am finished with this chicken soup, you gonna hear some scream!"

Marriage is not love; it is something else.

A woman at the grave of her husband was wailing,
"Oh, Joseph, it is four years since you have gone, but I
still miss you!"

Just then Grossberg passed by and saw the woman
crying. "Excuse me," he said, "who are you mourn-
ing?"

"My husband," she said. "I miss him so much!"

Grossberg looked at the stone and then said, "Your
husband? But it says on the gravestone 'Sacred to the
memory of Golda Kreps'."

"Oh, yes, he put everything in my name."

So be a little aware before you are trapped! Marriage
is a trap: you will be trapped by the woman and the
woman will be trapped by you. It is a mutual trap. And
then legally you are allowed to torture each other
forever. And particularly in this country, not only for
one life but for lives together! Divorce is not even
allowed after you are dead. Next life also you will get
the same wife, remember!

And the last question

Bhagwan,
What is going on?

Anand Subhuti,

I AM SURPRISED, because that's exactly what I was
going to ask you all! I don't know. But: *Not knowing is the most intimate.*

The ancients said:

*"(Self-)cultivation takes an unimaginable time
(While) enlightenment in an instant is attained."*

*If the training is efficient, enlightenment will
be attained in one fingersnap.*

*In days gone by, Ch'an Master Hui Chueh of Lang
Yeh mountain, had a disciple who called on him for
instruction. The Master taught her to examine into the
sentence: "Take no notice."*

*She followed his instruction strictly without
backsliding.*

*One day her house caught fire, but she said:
"Take no notice."*

*Another day, her son fell into the water and when
a bystander called her, she said: "Take no notice."*

*She observed exactly her Master's instruction by
laying down all casual thoughts.*

*One day, as her husband lit the fire to make fritters
of twisted dough, she threw into the pan full of boiling
(vegetable) oil a batter which made a noise.*

*Upon hearing the noise, she was instantly
enlightened. Then she threw the pan of oil on the
ground, clapped her hands and laughed.*

*Thinking she was insane, her husband scolded her
and said: "Why do you do this? Are you mad?"*

She replied: "Take no notice."

*Then she went to the Master Hui Chueh and asked
him to verify her achievement.*

*The Master confirmed that she had obtained the
holy fruit.*

Take
No Notice

THERE ARE TWO PATHS TO THE ULTIMATE TRUTH. The first is of self-cultivation and the second is of enlightenment. The first is basically wrong. It only appears to be a path; it is not. One goes on and on in circles, but one never arrives. The second does not appear to be a path because there is no space for a path when something happens instantly, when something happens immediately. When something happens without taking any time, how can there be a path?

This paradox has to be understood as deeply as possible: the first appears to be the path but is not; the second appears not to be a path but is. The first appears to be a path because there is infinite time; it is a time phenomenon. But anything happening in time cannot lead you beyond time; anything happening in time only strengthens time.

Time means mind. Time *is* a projection of mind. It does not exist; it is only an illusion. Only the present exists—and the present is not part of time. The present is part of eternity. Past is time, future is time; both are non-existential. The past is only memory and the future is only imagination; memory and imagination, both are non-existential. We create the past because we cling to memory; clinging to the memory is the source of the past. And we create the future because we have so many desires yet to be fulfilled, we have so many imaginations yet to be realized. And desires need a future like a screen onto which they can be projected.

Past and future are mind phenomena; and past and future make your whole idea of time. Ordinarily you think that time is divided into three divisions: past, present and future. That is totally wrong. That is not how the awakened ones have seen time. They say time consists only of two divisions: past and future. The present is not part of time at all; the present belongs to the beyond.

The first path—the path of self-cultivation—is a time path; it has nothing to do with eternity. And truth is eternity.

The second path—the path of enlightenment, Zen Masters have always called the pathless path because it does not appear to be a path at all. It cannot appear as a path, but just for the purposes of communication we will call it "the second path," arbitrarily. The second path is not part of time, it is part of eternity. Hence it happens instantaneously; it happens in the present. You cannot desire it, you cannot be ambitious for it.

On the first path, the false path, all is allowed. You can imagine, you can desire, you can be ambitious. You can change all your worldly desires into other-worldly desires. That's what the so-called religious people go on doing. They don't desire money any more—they are fed up with it, tired of it, frustrated with it, bored with it—but they start desiring God. Desire persists; it changes its object. Money is no more the object of desire but God; pleasure is no more the object of desire but bliss. But what bliss can you imagine? Whatsoever you imagine in the name of bliss is nothing but your idea of pleasure—maybe a little bit refined, cultivated, sophisticated, but it can't be more than that.

The people who stop desiring worldly things start desiring heaven and heavenly pleasures. But what are they?—magnified forms of the same old desires, in fact more dangerous than the worldly desires, because with the worldly desires one thing is absolutely certain: you are bound to get frustrated sooner or later. You will get out of them; you cannot remain in them forever. The very nature of them is such that they promise you, but they never fulfill their promises—the goods are never delivered. How long can you remain deceived by them? Even the *most* stupid person has glimpses, once in a while, that he is chasing illusions which cannot be fulfilled by the very nature of existence. The intelligent one comes to the realization sooner.

But with the other-worldly desires there is far greater danger because they are other-worldly, and to see them and to experience them you will have to wait till death. They will happen only after death so you cannot be free of them in life, while you are alive. And a man who has lived unconsciously his whole life, his death is going to be the culmination of unconsciousness; he will die in unconsciousness. In death also he will not be able to disillusion himself. And the person who dies in unconsciousness is born again in unconsciousness. It is a vicious circle; it goes on and on. And the person who is born in unconsciousness will repeat the same stupidities that he has been repeating for millions of lives.

Unless you become alert and aware *in* life, unless you change the quality of your living, you will not die consciously. And only a conscious death can bring you to a conscious birth; and then a far more conscious life opens its doors.

Changing worldly desires into other-worldly desires is the last strategy of the mind to keep you captive, to keep you a prisoner, to keep you in bondage.

So the first path is not really a path but a deception— but a very alluring deception. In the first place, it is *self*-cultivation. It is not against the ego; it is rooted in the refinement of the ego. Refine your ego of all grossness, then you become a self. The ego is like a raw diamond: you go on cutting it and polishing it and then it becomes a Kohinoor, very precious. That is your idea of "self," but it is nothing but ego with a beautiful name, with a spiritual flavor thrown in. It is the same old illusory ego.

The very idea that "I am" is wrong. The whole is, God is—I am not. Either I can exist or God can exist; we cannot both exist together—because if *I* exist, then I am a separate entity. Then I have my own existence independent of God. But God simply means the total, the whole. How can I be independent of it? How can I be separate from it? If I exist, I destroy the very idea of totality.

The people who deny God are the most egoistic people. It is not an accident that Friedrich Nietzsche declared God dead. He was one of the most egoistic persons possible. It was his ego that made him insane finally. Ego is insanity, the basic insanity, the most fundamental, out of which all other insanities arise. He said: "God is dead and man is free." That sentence is significant. In one sentence he has said the whole thing: Man can be free only if God is dead; if God is alive, then man cannot be free, in fact man cannot exist.

The very idea that "I am" is unspiritual. The idea of the self is unspiritual.

And what is self-cultivation? It is an effort to polish; it is an effort to create a beautiful character, to drop all that is unrespectable and to create all that is respectable. That's why in different countries different things are cultivated by the spiritual people—the so-called spiritual. It depends on the society; what the society respects, that will be cultivated.

In Soviet Russia, before the revolution, there was a Christian sect which believed that sexual organs should be cut, only then are you real Christians. The statement of Jesus was taken literally. Jesus has said: Be eunuchs of God. And these fools followed it literally. Every year they would gather in thousands and in a mad frenzy they would cut their sexual organs. Men would cut their genital organs, women would cut their breasts. And those who were able to do it were thought to be saints; they were very much respected—they had made a great sacrifice. Now, anywhere else they would have been thought utterly insane; but because in that particular society it was respected, they were saints.

In India you can find many people lying down on beds of thorns or needles, and they are thought to be great sages. If you look into their eyes, they are just stupid people. Lying down on a bed of thorns can't make one spiritual. It will simply deaden your body, your sensitivity. Your body will become more and more dull; it will not feel.

That's how it happens. Your face does not feel the cold because it remains open; it becomes insensitive to the cold. Your hands don't feel the cold so much because they are open; they become insensitive to the cold. Exactly in the same way you can live naked. Only for the beginning few months will you feel the cold; slowly slowly your body will adjust.

That's how the Jaina monks live naked. And their followers praise them like anything; they think: "This is what real spirituality is. Look, they have gone beyond the body!" They have gone nowhere; the body has just become dull. And when the body becomes dull it naturally creates a dullness of the mind too, because body and mind are deeply one. The body is the outer shell of the mind and the mind is the inner core of the body.

If you really want to be a sensitive, intelligent mind, you need a sensitive, intelligent body too. Yes, the body has its own intelligence. Don't kill it, don't destroy it, otherwise you will be destroying your intelligence. But if it is respected, then it becomes something religious, spiritual, holy.

Anything that the society respects becomes a nourishment for your ego. And people are ready to do any stupid thing. The only joy is that it will bring respectability.

Self-cultivation is nothing but another name for ego-cultivation. It is not a real path. In fact, no real path is needed. It looks like a long long, arduous path; it needs many lives. The people who have been preaching self-cultivation know perfectly well that one life is not enough; otherwise they will be exposed. So they imagine many many lives, a long, arduous journey of many lives. Then finally, after an unimaginable time, you arrive. In fact, you never arrive. You cannot arrive because you are already there. Hence this very idea of a path leading to a goal is meaningless.

Try to understand the paradox; it is very significant in understanding the spirit of Zen.

Z EN IS NOT A WAY, IS NOT A PATH. Hence they call it the gateless gate, the pathless path, the effortless effort, the actionless action. They use these contradictory terms just to point towards a certain truth: that a path means there is a goal and the goal has to be in the future. You are here, the goal is there, and between you and the goal a path is needed, a bridge, to join you. The very idea of a path means you have yet to arrive home, that you are not at home already.

The second path—the pathless path, the path of enlightenment—has a totally different revelation to make, a totally different declaration of immense value: that you are already it. *"Ah, this!"* There is nowhere to go, no need to go. There is *no one* to go. We are already enlightened. Then only can it happen in an instant—because it is a question of awakening.

For example, if you have fallen asleep and you are dreaming . . . you can dream that you are on the moon. Do you think that if somebody wakes you up you will have to come back from the moon? Then it will take time. If you have already reached the moon, then you will have to come back and it will take time. The airship may not be available right now. There may be no tickets available; it may be full. But you can be awakened because it is only a dream that you are on the moon. In fact you are in your bed, in your home;

you had not gone anywhere. Just a little shaking and you are suddenly back—back from your dreams.

The world is only a dream. We need not go anywhere; we have always been here; we *are* here and we are going to be here. But we can fall asleep and we can dream.

The All-Indian National Guard was out on maneuvers. They were about to begin a mock battle between the "red" team and the "blue" team when they received a telegram from Delhi: "Because of recent budget cuts we cannot supply weapons or ammunition, but please continue with your battle for training purposes."

The General called his troops together and said, "We will simulate the battle. If you are within a hundred yards of the enemy, point your arm and shout 'BANG-BANG' for a rifle. If you are within fifty feet, throw your arms over your head and shout 'BOOM' for a hand grenade. If you are within five feet, wave your arms and shout 'SLASH-SLASH' for a bayonet."

Private Abul was put on scout patrol, and apparently all the action went in another direction. He was out for three days and three nights, but did not see another person.

On the fourth day Abul was sitting under a tree, discouraged, when he saw a figure coming across the hill in his direction. He got down on his hands and knees and crawled through the mud and weeds, as he had been trained. Sure enough, it was a soldier from the other team.

Abul raised his arm and shouted "BANG-BANG!" but he got no response. So he ran up closer, threw his arm over his head, and shouted "BOOM!" very loudly. The other soldier did not even turn in his direction. So he ran right up to the soldier and shouted in his ear "SLASH-SLASH! SLASH-SLASH!" but still he got no reaction.

Abul was angry. He grabbed the other soldier by the arm and shouted, "Hey! You are not playing according to the rules. I went 'BANG-BANG,' I shouted 'BOOM,' and I came right up to you and said 'SLASH-SLASH,' and you have not even indicated that you have seen me yet."

At this point, the other soldier wheeled around to Abul and said in a deep voice, "RUMBLE-RUMBLE, I am a tank!"

This is the situation. You are not what you think you are, you are not what you believe you are. All your beliefs are dreams. Maybe you have been dreaming for so long that they appear almost like realities.

So the question is not of self-cultivation: the question is of enlightenment.

Zen believes in sudden enlightenment because Zen believes that you are already enlightened; just a certain situation is needed which can wake you up. Just a little alarm may do the work. If you are a little alert, just a little alarm and you are suddenly awake. And all the dream with all its long long desires, journeys, kingdoms, mountains, oceans. . . they have all disappeared in a single instant.

This beautiful story:

The ancients said:

"(Self-)cultivation   takes   an   unimaginable time. . . ."

It is bound to take an unimaginable time because you will be fighting with shadows. You cannot conquer them, you cannot destroy them either. In fact, the more you fight with them, the more you believe in their existence. If you fight with your own shadow, do you think there is any possibility of your ever becoming victorious? It's impossible. And it is not because the shadow is stronger than you that the victory is impossible. Just the contrary: the shadow has *no* power, it has *no* existence, and you start fighting with something which is non-existential—how can you win? You will be dissipating your energy. You will become tired and the shadow will remain unaffected. It will not get tired. You cannot kill it, you cannot burn it, you cannot even escape from it. The faster you run, the faster it comes behind you.

The only way to get rid of it is to *see* that it is not there at all. Seeing that a shadow is a shadow is liberation. Just seeing, no cultivation! And once the shadows disappear, your life has a luminosity of its own. Certainly there will arise great perfume, but it will not be something cultivated; it will not be something painted from the outside.

That's the difference between a saint and a sage. A saint follows the path of self-cultivation. He practices non-violence, like Mahatma Gandhi; he practices truth, truthfulness; he practices sincerity, honesty. But these are all practices. And whenever you are practicing non-violence, what are you doing? What is really happening inside you? You must be repressing violence. When you are practicing—when you *have* to practice—truth, what does it mean? It simply means untruth arises in you and you repress it and you go against it, and you say the truth. But the untruth has not disappeared from your being. You can push it downwards into the very basement of your being; you can throw it into the deep darkness of the unconscious. You can become completely oblivious of it. You can forget that it exists, but it exists and it is bound to function from those deep, dark depths of your being in such a subtle way that you will never be aware that you are still in its grip—in fact, far more so than before because when it was consciously felt you were not so much in its grip. Now the enemy has become hidden.

That's my observation of Mahatma Gandhi. He observed, cultivated non-violence; but I have looked deeply into his life and he is one of the most violent men this century has known. But his violence is very polished; his violence is so sophisticated that it looks almost like non-violence. And his violence has such subtle ways that you cannot detect it easily. It comes from the back door; it is never at the front door. You will not find it in his drawing-room; it is not there. It has started living somewhere in the servants' quarters at the back of the house where nobody ever goes, but it goes on pulling his strings from there.

For example, if ordinarily you are angry, you are angry with the person who has provoked it. Mahatma Gandhi would be angry with himself, not with the person. He would turn his anger upon himself; he would make it introverted. Now it is very difficult to detect it. He would go on a fast, he would become suicidal, he would start torturing himself. And in a subtle way he would torture the other by torturing himself.

In his ashram, if somebody was found drinking tea . . . . Now tea is so innocent, but it was a sin in Mahatma Gandhi's ashram. These ashrams exist by creating guilt in people; they don't miss any opportunity to create guilt. That is their trade-secret, so no opportunity has to be missed. Even tea is enough; it has to be used. If somebody is found drinking tea, he is a sinner. He is committing a crime—far more than a crime, because a sin is something far deeper than a crime. If somebody was found. . . .

And people used to drink tea. They would drink tea in hiding; they had to hide. Just to drink tea they had to be thieves, deceivers, hypocrites! That's what your so-called religions have done to millions of people. Rather than making them spiritual they have simply made them, reduced them to hypocrites.

They would pretend that they didn't drink tea, but once in a while they would be found red-handed. And Gandhi was searching, looking; he had agents planted to find out who was going against the rules. And whenever somebody was found he would be called . . . and Gandhi would go on a fast to punish himself.

"What kind of logic is this?" you will ask. It is a very simple logic. In India it has been followed for centuries. The trick is that Gandhi used to say, "I must not yet be a perfect Master, that's why a disciple can deceive me. So I must purify myself. You could deceive me because I am not yet perfect. If I was perfect nobody could deceive me. How can you imagine deceiving a perfect Master? So there is some imperfection in me."

Look at the humbleness! And he would torture himself; he would go on a fast. Now Gandhi is fasting because you have taken a cup of tea. How will *you* feel? His three days' fast for you, just for a single cup of tea! It will be too heavy on you. If he had hit you on the head it would not have been so heavy. If he had insulted you, punished you, told you to go on a fast for three days, it would have been far simpler—and far more compassionate. But the old man himself is fasting, torturing himself, and you are condemned by every eye in the ashram. Everybody is looking at you as a great sinner: "It is because of *you* that the Master is suffering. And just for a cup of tea? How low you have fallen!"

And the person would go and touch his feet and cry and weep, but Gandhi wouldn't listen. He had to purify himself.

This is all violence; I don't call it non-violence. It is violence with a vengeance, but in such a subtle way that it is very difficult to detect. Even Gandhi may not have been aware at all of what he was doing—because he was not practicing awareness, he was practicing non-violence.

You can go on practicing . . . then there are a thousand and one things to be practiced. And when will you be able to get out of all that is wrong in your life? It will take an unimaginable time. And then, too, do you think you will be out of it? It is not possible; you will not be out of it.

I have never seen anybody arriving at truth by self-cultivation. In fact, the people who go for self-cultivation are not very intelligent people because they have missed the most fundamental insight: that we are not going anywhere, that God is not something to be achieved; God is already the *case* in you. You are pregnant with God, you are made of the stuff called God. Nothing has to be achieved—only a certain awareness, a *self*-awareness.

There is an unusual store in New York where one can buy exotic foods from all over the world.

Mulla Nasruddin visited this store recently. He found rare tropical fruits from the jungles of South America and many strange delicacies from Africa and the Middle East.

In one corner he found a counter with several trays of human brains. There were politicians' brains at $1 per pound, engineers' brains at $2 per pound, and there was one tray of saints' brains at $50 per pound.

Since all the brains looked very much alike, he asked the man behind the counter, "Why do you charge so much more for the saints' brains?"

The man peered out from behind his glasses and answered, "Do you have any idea how many saints we have to go through to get a pound of brains?"

My observation of your so-called saints is exactly the same. I don't think they are very intelligent people—basically stupid, because unless one is stupid one cannot follow the path of self-cultivation. It *appears* only as a path; it is not. And it is tedious and it is long; in fact, it is unending.

You can change one habit; it will start asserting itself in something else. You can close one door and another door immediately opens. By the time you close that door a third door is bound to open—because basically you remain the same, the same old unconscious person. Trying to be humble you will be simply becoming more and more egoistic and nothing else. Your humbleness will be simply a new way of fulfilling your ego. Deep down you will imagine yourself to be the humblest person in the world—there is nobody who is more humble than you. Now, this is ego speaking a new language, but the meaning is the same. The language is changed but the meaning is the same; translated into a different language it does not change. First you were the greatest man in the world, now you are the humblest man in the world, but you remain special, you remain extraordinary, you remain superior. First you were this, now you are that, but deep down nothing has changed. Nothing can ever change by self-cultivation.

A man spent thousands of dollars going from doctor to doctor trying to find a cure for his insomnia. Finally a doctor was able to help him.

"You must be terribly relieved," said one of his friends sympathetically.

"You said it!" replied the former insomniac. "Why, sometimes I lie awake all night thinking of how I used to suffer."

So what has changed? Self-cultivation only gives you a deception: the deception that something is happening, that you are doing something, that something great is on the way; that if not today, tomorrow it is going to happen.

Hornstein manufactured coats, but business was so bad the poor man could not sleep.

"Count sheep," advised Slodnick, his friend. "It is the best-known cure."

"What can I lose?" said Hornstein. "I will try tonight."

The next morning he looked more bleary-eyed than ever.

"What happened?" asked Slodnick.

"Sheep I could count," moaned Hornstein. "I counted up to fifty thousand. Then I sheared the sheep and made up fifty thousand overcoats. Then came the problem that kept me awake all the rest of the night: where could I get fifty thousand linings?''

No such things are going to help because if the *mind* is the same, it will go on creating the same problem in different ways. Basically the roots have to be transformed; just pruning the leaves is not going to help. And self-cultivation is only pruning of the leaves.

The ancients said:

"(Self-)cultivation takes an unimaginable time (While) enlightenment in an instant is attained."

E NLIGHTENMENT IS ATTAINED IN A SINGLE MOMENT. Why?—because you are already enlightened. You have simply forgotten it. You have to be reminded, that's all.

The function of the Master is to remind you, not to give you a path but to give you a remembrance; not to give you methods of cultivation, not to give you a character, virtue, but only awareness, intelligence, awakening.

In a single moment it can be attained because you have never lost it in the first place. You are dreaming that you are unenlightened. You can dream you are in heaven, you can dream you are in hell. And you know! —you dream sometimes you are in heaven and sometimes in hell. In the morning you can be in heaven and by the evening you can be in hell. One moment you can be in heaven, another moment you can be in hell. It all depends on you. It is something to do with your psyche; it is not something outside you.

A man died, arrived at the Pearly Gates, and was

shown by St. Peter to a waiting room. He sat there, naturally anxious to know whether he would be sent to Heaven or to Hell. The door opened and a famous saint walked in.

The man rejoiced, "I must be in Heaven!"

Just then the door opened again and a famous prostitute walked in. The man was confused. "In that case I must be in Hell!" he thought.

While he was still wondering, the saint grabbed the prostitute and started making love to her. The man, flabbergasted, ran to St. Peter and asked, "You *must* tell me: is this Heaven or Hell?"

"Can't you see?" answered St. Peter. "It is Heaven for him and Hell for her!"

Heaven and hell are not geographical; they are not something outside you, they are something that belongs to your interiority. If you are awake, then you are in a totally different universe; it is as if in your awakening the whole existence becomes awakened. It takes a new color, a new flavor, a new fragrance. When you are asleep, the whole existence sleeps with you. It *all* depends on you.

So the question is not of cultivating any character, of becoming virtuous, of becoming a saint. The question is how to come out of dreams, how to come out of the past and the future, how to be just herenow.

That's what enlightenment is . . . *"Ah, this!"*

When Alice was at the Mad Hatter's tea party, she noticed that no jam was available. She asked for jam, and the Mad Hatter said, "Jam is served every other day."

Alice protested, "But there was no jam yesterday either!"

"That's right," said the Mad Hatter. "The rule is: always jam yesterday and jam tomorrow, never jam today . . . because today is not every other day!"

And that's how you are living: jam yesterday, jam tomorrow, never jam today. And that's where jam is! So you only imagine; you go on in a drugged, sleepy state. You have forgotten completely that this moment is the *only* real moment there is. And if you want to have any contact with reality, wake up herenow!

Hence this strange idea of Zen that enlightenment happens in an instant. Many people become puzzled: "How can it happen in an instant?" Indians particularly become very puzzled because they have the idea that first you have to get rid of all the past karmas, and now this foolish idea has reached to the West. Now in the West people are talking about past karma: first you have to get rid of the past karma.

Do you know how long the past is? It is eternity! And if you are to get rid of all past karma you are never going to get rid of it—that much is certain. And meanwhile you will be creating other karmas, and the past will go on becoming bigger and bigger every day. If that is the only way out—that one has to get rid of all past karmas—then there is no possibility of enlightenment. Then there has never been any Buddha and there is never going to be any Buddha; it is impossible. Just think of all the past lives and all the karmas that you have built up—first you have to get rid of them. And how are you going to get rid of them? In trying to get rid of them you will have to create other karmas. And this is a vicious circle.

"And to be totally enlightened," the people who believe in the philosophy of karma say, "not only are you to get rid of the bad karmas, you have to get rid of the good karmas too—because bad karmas create iron chains and good karmas create golden chains. But chains are chains, and you have to get rid of all kinds of chains." Now things become even more complicated. And how can you get rid of bad karmas? If you ask them they say, "Create good karma to get rid of bad karmas." And how can you get rid of good karmas? Then the saints become angry. They say, "Stop! You are arguing too much. This is not a question of argument. Believe, trust, have faith!"

It is not really a question of getting rid of karmas. When in the morning you wake up, do you have to get rid of all the dreams first? You have been a thief in the dreams, a murderer, a rapist, or a saint . . . you can be all kinds of things in a dream. Do you have to get rid of all those dreams first? The *moment* you are awake you are out of all those dreams—they are finished! There is no question of getting rid of them.

That is the essential message of Zen: that you need not be worried about the past karmas; they were all dream acts. Just wake up and they are all finished.

But we are sleepy people and anything that fits with our sleep has great appeal. We listen only according to our state of mind. The whole world is asleep. There is rarely, once in a while, a person who is not asleep, who is awake. When he speaks to you there is misunderstanding, obviously. He speaks from his standpoint, from his awakening, and he says, "Forget all about your dreams—that is all nonsense! Good and bad, they are all alike; saint and sinner, they are all alike. Simply wake up! Don't be worried that first you have to become a saint in your dream, that you have to change your being a sinner into being a saint first, then you can wake up. Why go by such a long route? You can wake up directly! You can wake up while you are committing a sin; while you are murdering somebody in your dream you can wake up. There is no problem.

In fact, if you are a saint you may not like to wake up. A murderer will find it easier to wake up because he has nothing to lose, but the saint has great prestige to lose. Maybe he is being garlanded and a Nobel prize is being given and people are clapping and touching his feet . . . and suddenly the alarm goes. Is this the time for the alarm? Can't the alarm wait a little more? When things are going so sweetly and beautifully the alarm can wait a little. A murderer has nothing to lose. He is already suffering; he is in a deep inner torture. In fact, he will feel relieved if the alarm goes off. He will feel a great freedom coming out of that nightmare.

Hence it happens more often that sinners wake up earlier than the saints, because the sinners go through nightmares and saints are having such sweet dreams. Who wants to wake up when you are a king with a golden palace and enjoying all kinds of things? Maybe you are in paradise in your dream.

But one thing is certain: when you are asleep you have a certain language—the language of sleep—and you can understand other people who are asleep and speak the same language. That's why the philosophy of karma became so important, so prevalent, so dominant. It has ruled almost all the religions of the world in different ways.

In India there have been three great religions: Hinduism, Jainism, Buddhism. They disagree on every point *except* on the philosophy of karma; they disagree on *every* point possible. They disagree on the existence of

God, they disagree even on the existence of the soul,
they disagree on the existence of the world, but they
don't disagree on the philosophy of karma. It must
have some deep appeal for the sleeping mind. And
these people cannot understand Zen.

When a Hindu pundit or a Jaina *muni* comes to me
he is very much puzzled. He says, "Are you teaching instant, sudden enlightenment? Then what about Mahavira who had to struggle for many many lives to
become enlightened?"

I say to them, "Those stories are invented by you.
The Mahavira that *you* talk about is an invention of
your dream; you don't know about the real Mahavira.
How can you know about his past lives? You don't
even know about *your* past lives!" And there is not
even any agreement on his last life amongst his followers—what to say about his past lives?

On such factual matters . . . for example, whether he
was married or not: one sect of Jainas says he was not
married, because to them a man like Mahavira getting
married looks insulting, humiliating. And the other sect
of the Jainas says he was not only married, but he had a
daughter too. Now that is going too far—having a
daughter! That means he must have indulged in sex—
because at that time the story of Jesus had not happened. Virgin birth was not yet known!

They can't agree . . . the disciples can't agree about
Mahavira's last life on factual matters like marriage,
daughter, etcetera, and they talk about his past lives!

Anything that helps you to go on sleeping, postponing, appeals. "Even Mahavira had to work hard for
many many lives, so how can *we* become enlightened
in this life? It will take many lives, so there is no need to
do anything right now. We can wait! And it is *not* going

to happen right now anyway; it will take many many lives. Meanwhile, why not do other things? Accumulate more money, prestige, power. Do other things: eat, drink, be merry—because this is not going to happen, this enlightenment, right now; it will take many many lives. And meanwhile you cannot just go on sitting and waiting; one has to do something."

Sleeping people can understand a language which appeals to their sleep. We understand only that which triggers some process in our being.

The Sisters of Mercy were about to be sent as missionaries out into the world of sin. Mother Superior had one last question to ask each nun before deciding which of them were best fitted for the hazardous tasks ahead.

"Sister Agatha," she asked the first. "What would you do if you were walking along a deserted street at night and a strange man approached you and made indecent advances?"

"Oh, Holy Mother of God!" gasped the nun. "May all the saints forbid! Why, I would get down on my knees and pray to the Holy Virgin that my soul might be saved."

Mother Superior noted that Sister Agatha might be better suited to more domestic work.

The same question was asked of Sister Agnes, who replied, "Why, I would punch him in the nose . . . and then start running down the street as fast as I could, shouting 'Help, help!' "

Mother Superior noted Sister Agnes as one of the possible candidates for the missionary work.

Next she asked Sister Theresa, who began, "Well, first I would pull his trousers down. . . ." Mother

Superior choked a little, but Sister Theresa continued. "And then I would pull my dress up, and then...."

"Sister Theresa," interrupted the senior nun. "Now what kind of an answer is that?"

"Well," said the other, "I just figure that I can run faster with my dress up than he can with his trousers down!"

We understand only that which we *can* understand. The sleeping humanity can understand only certain things; it can *hear* only certain things. The other things are not heard or even if heard they are not understood; they are misunderstood.

Zen has been misunderstood very much. You will be surprised to know that even Buddhists don't understand Zen.

Many orthodox Buddhists have come to me asking why I emphasize Zen so much, because it is not the main Buddhist tradition. That is true; the main Buddhist tradition is against Zen. Zen seems to be a little outlandish, a little eccentric, for the simple reason that it brings such a totally new truth to you: *instant* enlightenment. Never has any other religion emphasized it so much: that you are capable of becoming enlightened right now—it is all up to you.

*If the training is efficient, enlightenment
will be attained in one fingersnap.*

There is no path as such, but there is a certain discipline to wake you up. That is called "training." Training has nothing to do with your character but something to do with your consciousness. Training simply means a certain space, a certain context has to be created around you in which awakening is easier than falling asleep—

just like when you want somebody to be awake you throw cold water into his eyes. Not that you teach him to be virtuous, not that you teach him to be non-violent—those things are not going to help him to be awake. But cold water, that is a totally different pheno-menon; that is creating a context. Or you give him a cup of tea; that helps him to wake up. Or you tell him to jog, run, shout; that will help him to wake up more quickly.

All Zen methods are like that: cold water thrown in your eyes, a hammer hit on your head. Zen is totally different from other religions. It does not give you a certain character; it certainly gives you a context.

In days gone by, Ch'an Master Hui Chueh
of Lang Yeh mountain, had a woman disciple
who called on him for instruction. The Master
taught her to examine into the sentence:
"Take no notice."

NOW, THIS IS CREATING A CONTEXT. The Master told her to meditate on this small sentence: "Take no notice." And it has to be meditated on in different situ-ations, in all possible situations. It has not to be forgot-ten *any* time; it has to be remembered continuously, whatsoever happens.

She followed his instruction strictly without
backsliding.

One day her house caught fire, but she
said: "Take no notice."

Now, this is creating a context. This is real training, this is discipline. The house is on fire and she remem-bers the instruction: "Take no notice." It is easy when the house is not on fire and everything is running smoothly, well, and you can sit silently in a small corner you have made in the house to meditate—then you can say, "Take no notice." It is easy, but it is not going to wake you up; it may even help you to fall asleep. But when the house is on fire it is difficult, very difficult. Your possessiveness is at stake, your life is in danger, your security is gone, your safety is gone. You may be just a beggar the next day on the street with nothing left.

But the woman must have been a real disciple.

She said: "Take no notice."

And not only did she say it, she *took* no notice. She relaxed, as if nothing was happening. And the moment you can see your house on fire and can see it as if nothing is happening, nothing happens. The house will be burned, but you will come out of that experience for the first time with clarity, with no dust on your mirror, with great insight. Everything is on fire! The whole life is on fire because we are dying every moment. Nothing is secure, nothing is safe. We only go on believing that everything is secure and safe. In this world of flux and change, where death is the ultimate end of everything, how can there be any security?

If you can see your own house on fire and go on meditating silently, relaxedly, in a deep let-go—*take no notice*—you will come out of it a totally different person, with a new consciousness, reborn.

Another day, her son fell into the
water and when a bystander called her, she
said, "Take no notice."

Now even more difficult—because a house is, after all,

a dead thing. We can make another house, money can be earned again. But your son falls into the water, is drowning. . . this is a more difficult situation, more attachment—your own son. And for the mother, the son is her extension, part of her, part of her soul, of her being. Still she says, "Take no notice."

She observed exactly her Master's instruction
by laying down all casual thoughts.

If this is possible . . . because these are the two problems in the world: possessiveness of things and relationship with people. These are *your* problems too. That's where people are asleep: either they are possessive with things or they are in heavy relationships with people. These are the two points which keep you clouded, confused, unaware.

She passed both the tests. And if you can pass these two things: if you can become aware that you possess nothing. . . . Use everything but possess nothing, and relate with people but don't become part of any relationship.

Relating is one thing, relationship quite another. Relating does not take you into any bondage; relationship is a bondage. Love people, but don't be jealous, don't be possessive. Relate with as many people as possible, but remain free and let them also be free of you. Don't try to dominate and don't allow anybody to dominate you either.

Use things, but remember: you come into the world with empty hands and you will go from the world again with empty hands, so you cannot possess anything.

If these two insights become clear and you start tak-

ing no note, all casual thoughts will disappear from
your mind. And all thoughts are casual, no thought is
essential. The essential is silence; thoughts are all
casual. When thoughts disappear, the essential sur-
faces. Great silence explodes in a tremendous melody.
And that experience is liberating, that experience is
divine.

> *One day, as her husband lit the fire*
> *to make fritters of twisted dough, she threw*
> *into the pan full of boiling (vegetable) oil*
> *a batter which made a noise.*

> *Upon hearing the noise, she was*
> *instantly enlightened.*

THAT'S WHAT I CALL . . . if you are ready, if the context is ready, then *anything* can trigger the process of enlightenment—*anything.* Just:

> *Upon hearing the noise, she was*
> *instantly enlightened.*

Nothing special was happening, just an ordinary noise.
You come across that kind of noise every day many
times. But if the right context is there, you are in a right
space . . . and she *was* in a right space: non-possessive,
unrelated to anything, to any person, non-dominating.
She was in a state of liberation, just on the borderline.
One step more and she would move into the world of
the Buddhas. And that small step can be caused by
anything whatsoever.

> *Upon hearing the noise. . . .*

That noise became the last alarm, the last straw on the
back of the camel.

. . . she was instantly enlightened. Then she
threw the pan of oil on the ground, clapped
her hands and laughed.

Why did she do that: *clapped her hands and laughed?*
When one becomes enlightened, laughter is almost a
natural by-product; spontaneously it comes—for the
simple reason that we have been searching and searching for lives for something which was already there inside. Our whole effort was ridiculous! Our whole effort
was absurd. One laughs at the great cosmic joke. One
laughs at the sense of humor that God must have or the
existence: that we have it with us already and we are
searching for it. One laughs at one's own ridiculous efforts, long long journeys, pilgrimages, for something
which was never lost in the first place. Hence the laughter, hence the clapping.

Thinking she was insane, her husband
scolded her and said. . . .

And of course, anybody who is still asleep seeing
somebody suddenly becoming enlightened, clapping
hands and laughing, is bound to think that the person
has gone insane. This *breakthrough* will look to the
sleeping person like a break*down;* it is not a break-
down. But the sleeping person can't help it; he can
understand only according to his values, criterions.

. . . he scolded her and said: "Why do you do
this? Are you mad?"

She replied: "Take no notice."

She continues: her meditation is still there. She is
following her Master's instruction to the very end. The

husband is calling her mad and she says: "Take no notice."

The world *will* call you mad. The world has always been calling Buddhas mad. Take no notice. It is natural; it should be accepted as a matter of course.

Then she went to Master Hui Chueh and asked him to verify her achievement.

THE MASTER'S FUNCTIONS ARE MANY. First: to help you to wake up, to provoke you into an awakening; to create the situation in which sleep becomes more and more difficult and awakening becomes more and more easy; and when for the first time you *are* awakened, to confirm it, because it is very difficult for the person himself. The territory is so unknown. The ego is lost, all old values are gone, the old mind is no more functioning. Everything is so new; nothing seems to be continuous with the old. There seems to be no way to judge, evaluate, be certain. One *is* in deep awe and wonder. One does not know what is happening, what has happened, what it is all about. One is simply at a loss.

Hence the last function of the Master is to confirm, to say, "Yes, this is it."

The Master confirmed that she had obtained the holy fruit.

Zen people call this "the holy fruit," the fruition, the flowering—coming to the ultimate awakening, coming to the ultimate experience of yourself and existence. But remember: it can only happen in the moment. It can only happen in the instant. It can only happen now—now or never.

You will ask: "Then why all these methods, train-ings?" They are just to bring you back to the now. You have gone too far away in the memories and in imagin-ation. They are not to create any cultivation; they are not for self-cultivation but for bringing you back home.

Here we are using all kinds of methods, and as many more people will be coming we will be devising new methods, because different people will need different methods. In the new commune we are going to have all possible methods. It has never been tried on such a scale. Every religion has a few methods, but we are go-ing to have *all* the methods of all the religions of the past and of all the religions that are going to happen in the future. We are going to create a space for *all* kinds of people, not for any particular type. The old religions are missing in that way.

For example, only a particular type of person can be helped by Mahavira's methods—only the type who be-longs to Mahavira's type can be helped. It is a very limited methodology. Mahavira attained to the holy fruit; he taught the same method by which he attained. Jesus had his own method, Mohammed had his own method. So no religion of the past could be universal because it belonged to a certain type and only that type could be benefited by it.

Hence one problem has arisen: you may be born in a Jaina family and you may not be of the same type which the Jaina method can help. Then you are in a dif-ficulty; your whole life will be a wastage. You will try the method; it won't suit you—and you will not change your method. You will think it is because of your past karmas that the method is not working, that it will take time. You will rationalize. You may be born in a Hindu family and Hindu methods may not work.

There are so many types of people in the world, and as the world has grown and people's consciousnesses have grown, more and more new types, more and more crossbreeds have come into existence which were never there before—which never existed in Mahavira's time, which never existed in Krishna's time. There are many new types, crossbreeds. And in the future this is going to happen more and more; the world is becoming a small village.

My effort is to use all the methods of the past, to make them up-to-date, to make them contemporary, and to create new methods for the future—for the future of humanity. Hence what I am teaching is neither Hinduism nor Buddhism nor Christianity, and yet I am teaching the essence of all the religions.

You are here not to cultivate a certain spiritual ego but to dissolve all the ego, to dissolve all sleep. You are here to wake up. The situation is being created—use this situation as totally as possible.

Remember this woman who was meditating on "Take no notice." Such totality is needed. The house is on fire and she says: "Take no notice." Her son falls into the water and she says: "Take no notice." Her husband calls her mad and she says: "Take no notice." Then such a simple meditation—of taking no notice—creates the necessary milieu in which she becomes aflame, afire. Her inner being explodes. She is no more the same old person; she is reborn. She is reborn as enlightened. She becomes a Buddha.

You are all Buddhas—sleeping, dreaming, but you are Buddhas all the same. My function is not to *make* Buddhas out of you, because you are already that, but just to help you remember it, to remind you.

Not Knowing is the Most Intimate

The first question

Bhagwan,
Is awareness a higher value than love?

Virendra,

THE HIGHEST PEAK IS THE CULMINATION of all the values: truth, love, awareness, authenticity, totality. At the highest peak they are indivisible. They are separate only in the dark valleys of our unconsciousness. They are separate only when they are polluted, mixed with other things. The moment they become pure they become one; the more pure, the closer they come to each other.

For example, each value exists on many planes; each value is a ladder of many rungs. Love is lust—the lowest rung, which touches hell; and love is also prayer —the highest rung, which touches paradise. And between these two there are many planes easily discernible.

In lust, love is only one percent; ninety-nine percent are other things: jealousies, ego trips, possessiveness, anger, sexuality. It is more physical, more chemical; it has nothing deeper than that. It is very superficial, not even skin-deep.

As you go higher, things become deeper; they start having new dimensions. That which was only physiological starts having a psychological dimension to it. That which was nothing but biology starts becoming psychology. We share biology with all the animals; we don't share psychology with all the animals.

When love goes still higher—or deeper, which is the same—then it starts having something of the spiritual in it. It becomes metaphysical. Only Buddhas, Krishnas, Christs, they know that quality of love.

Love is spread all the way and so are other values. When love is one hundred percent pure you cannot make any distinction between love and awareness; then they are no more two. You cannot make any distinction between love and God even; they are no more two. Hence Jesus' statement that God is love. He makes them synonymous. There is great insight in it.

On the periphery everything appears separate from everything else; on the periphery existence is many. As you come closer to the center, the manyness starts melting, dissolving, and oneness starts arising. At the center, everything is one.

Hence your question, Virendra, is right only if you don't understand the highest quality of love and awareness. It is absolutely irrelevant if you have any glimpse of the Everest, of the highest peak.

You ask: *Is awareness a higher value than love?*

There is nothing higher and nothing lower. In fact,

there are not two values at all. These are the two paths
from the valley leading to the peak. One path is of
awareness, meditation: the path of Zen we have been
talking about these days. And the other is the path of
love, the path of the devotees, the *bhaktas,* the Sufis.
These two paths are separate when you start the journey; you have to choose. Whichever you choose is going to lead to the same peak. And as you come closer to
the peak you will be surprised: the travelers on the
other path are coming closer to you. Slowly slowly, the
paths start merging into each other. By the time you
have reached the ultimate, they are one.

The person who follows the path of awareness finds
love as a consequence of his awareness, as a by-
product, as a shadow. And the person who follows the
path of love finds awareness as a consequence, as a by-
product, as a shadow of love. They are two sides of the
same coin.

And remember: if your awareness lacks love then it is
still impure; it has not yet known one hundred percent
purity. It is not yet *really* awareness; it must be mixed
with unawareness. It is not pure light; there must be
pockets of darkness inside you still working, functioning, influencing you, dominating you. If your love is
without awareness, then it is not love yet. It must be
something lower, something closer to lust than to
prayer.

So let it be a criterion: if you follow the path of
awareness, let love be the criterion. When your awareness suddenly blooms into love, know perfectly well
that awareness has happened, *samadhi* has been
achieved. If you follow the path of love, then let awareness function as a criterion, as a touchstone. When suddenly, from nowhere, at the very center of your love, a

flame of awareness starts arising, know perfectly well
. . . rejoice! You have come home.

The second question

*Why, Bhagwan, isn't knowledge of the
scriptures helpful in finding the truth?*

Maneeshi,

KNOWLEDGE IS NOT YOURS, THAT'S WHY. It is borrowed. And can you borrow truth? Truth is un-
transferable; nobody can give it to you. Not even an
alive Master can transmit it to you. You can learn, but it
cannot be taught. So what to say about dead scriptures,
howsoever holy they may be? They must have come
from some original source; some Master, someone
awakened must have been at the very source of them—
but now they are only words. They are only words
about truth, information about truth.

To be with Krishna is a totally different matter from
reading the Bhagavad Gita. To be with Mohammed, attuned, in deep harmony, overlapping with his being,
allowing his being to stir and move your heart, is one
thing. And just to read the Koran is a far, faraway cry; it
is an echo in the mountains. It is not the truth itself; it is
a reflection, a full moon reflected in the lake. If you
jump into the lake you are not going to get to the
moon; in fact, if you jump into the lake even the reflection will disappear. Scriptures are only mirrors reflecting faraway truths.

Now the Vedas have existed for at least five thousand
years; they reflect something five thousand years old.

Much dust has gathered on the mirror, much interpretation, commentary—that's what I mean by dust. Now you cannot know exactly what the Vedas say; you know only the commentators, the interpreters, and they are thousands. There is a thick wall of commentaries and it is impossible to just put it aside. You will know only *about* truth, and not only that: you will know commentaries and interpretations of people who have not experienced at all.

Knowledge is imparted for other purposes. Yes, there is a possibility of imparting knowledge about the world because the world is outside you, it is objective. Science is knowledge; science, the very word, means exactly knowledge. But religion is not knowledge.

Religion is experience—for the simple reason that its whole concern is your interiority, your subjectivity, which is available only to you and to nobody else. You cannot invite even your beloved into your inner being. There you are utterly alone—and there resides the truth.

Knowledge will go on enhancing, decorating, enriching your memory, but not your being. Your being is a totally different phenomenon. In fact, knowledge will create barriers. One has to unlearn all that one has learned—only then does one reach the being. One has to be innocent. *Not knowing is the most intimate.* Knowing creates distance.

You ask me, Maneeshi: *Why isn't knowledge of the scriptures helpful in finding the truth?*

For the simple reason that if you accumulate knowledge you will be starting to believe in conclusions. You will already conclude what truth is without *knowing* it, and your conclusion will become the greatest hindrance.   Truth has to be approached in utter nudity, in utter purity, in silence, in a state of innocence, child-like wonder and awe; not knowing already, not full of the rubbish called knowledge, not full of the Vedas and the Bibles and the Korans, but utterly silent . . . without any thought, without any conclusion, without knowing anything about truth. When you approach in this way, suddenly truth is revealed. And truth is revealed here and now: *"Ah, this!"* A great rejoicing starts happening inside you.

Truth is not separate from you; it is your innermost core. So you need not to learn it from somebody else. Then what's the function of the Masters?

The function of the Masters is to help you drop your knowledge, to help you unlearn, to help you towards a state of unconditioning. Your knowledge means you will be always looking through a curtain and that curtain will distort everything. And knowledge is dead. Consciousness is needed, knowing is needed, a state of seeing is needed, but not knowledge. How can you know the alive through the dead?

A man stepped into a very crowded bus. After a while he took out his glass eye, threw it up in the air, then put it back in again. Ten minutes later he again took out his glass eye, threw it up in the air, then put it back in again.

The lady next to him was horrified. "What are you doing?" she cried.

"I am just trying to see if there is any room up front."

That's what knowledge is: a glass eye. You cannot see through it, it is impossible to see through it.

Drop all your conclusions—Hindu, Christian, Mohammedan, Jaina, Jewish. Drop all the knowledge that has been forced upon you. Every child has been poisoned—poisoned by knowledge, poisoned by the parents, the society, the church, the state. Every child has been distracted from his innocence, from his not-knowing. And that's why every child, slowly slowly, becomes so burdened that he loses all joy of life, all ecstasy of being, and he becomes just like the crowd, part of the crowd.

In fact, the moment a child is perfectly conditioned by you, you are very happy; you call it "religious education." You are very happy that the child has been initiated into the religion of his parents. All that you have done is you have destroyed his capacity to know on his own. You have destroyed his authenticity. You have destroyed his very precious innocence. You have closed his doors and windows. Now he will live an encapsulated existence. He will live in his inner darkness, surrounded by all kinds of stupid theories, systems of thought, philosophies, ideologies. He will be lost in a jungle of words and he will not be able to come out of it easily.

Even if he comes across a Master, if he meets a Buddha, then too it will take years for him to unlearn—because learning becomes almost your blood, your bones, your marrow. And to go against your own knowledge seems to be going against yourself, against your tradition, against your country, against your religion. It seems as if you are a traitor, as if you are betraying. In fact, your society has betrayed you, has contaminated your soul.

Every society has been doing that up to now, and every society has been very successfully doing it. That's why it is so rare to find a Buddha; it is so rare to escape from the traps the society puts all around the child. And the child is so unaware; he can easily be conditioned, hypnotized. And that's what goes on and on in the temples, in the churches, in the schools, colleges, universities. They all serve the past; they don't serve the future. Their function is to perpetuate the past, the dead past.

My work here is just the opposite. I am not here to perpetuate the past; hence I am against all knowledge. I am all for learning, but learning means innocence, learning means openness, learning means receptivity. Learning means a non-egoistic approach towards reality. Learning means: "I don't know and I am ready— ready to know." Knowledge means: "I know already." Knowledge is the greatest deception that society creates in people's minds.

My function is to serve the future, not the past. The past is no more, but the future is coming every moment. I want you to become innocent, seers, knowers —not knowledgeable—alert, aware, not unconsciously clinging to conclusions.

The third question

Bhagwan,
Why does it take so long for me to get it?

Pankaja,

IT IS BECAUSE OF YOUR KNOWLEDGE. Pankaja has written many books; she has been a well-known author. And here I have given her the work of cleaning. In the beginning it was very hurtful to her ego. She must have been hoping some day to get a Nobel prize!

And she has been wondering what she is doing here. Her books have been praised and appreciated, and rather than giving her some work nourishing to her ego I have given her very ego-shattering work: cleaning the toilets of the ashram. It was difficult for her to swallow, but she is a courageous soul, she swallowed it. And slowly slowly she has become relaxed.

Pankaja, it is not special to you; it takes time for everybody. And the more successful you have been in life, the more it takes for you to get it, because your very success is nothing but a prop, a new prop for the ego—and ego is the barrier. The ego has to be shattered, uprooted totally, smashed, burned, so nothing remains of it. It is arduous work, hard work.

And sometimes it looks as if the Master is cruel. But the Master has to be cruel because he loves you, because he has compassion for you. It may appear paradoxical in the beginning—because if you have compassion, then you can't be cruel. That is the complexity of the work: that if the Master is really compassionate he cannot sympathize with anything that nourishes your ego.

So I have been in every way shattering Pankaja's ego. She has been crying and weeping and freaking out . . . but slowly slowly things have settled. The storm is no more and a great silence has come in.

In fact, if you think of your many past lives—such a long long sleep, such a long long dreaming—then just being here with me for two, three years is not a long time if the silence has started permeating your being. Even if it happens in thirty years' time it is happening soon.

Many people come to me and ask, "Bhagwan, when is *my* satori going to happen?"

I say, "Very soon"—but remember what I mean by "very soon." It may take thirty years, forty years, fifty years, but that is very soon. Looking at your long long journey of darkness, if within thirty years we can create the light it is really as fast as it can be.

But things are happening far more quickly. Every situation is being created here so processes can be quickened. It is not too late, Pankaja, it is too early. And I can see the change happening. The spring is not far away; the first flowers have already appeared.

In fact, this was your vocation, but it took so many years of your life to reach me. What you were doing before you came to me was not really part of your heart; it was just a head trip—hence it was not a fulfillment. Successful you could become; famous, yes, that was possible. But it would not have been a contentment, it would not have been a deep deep joy—because unless something that belongs to your heart starts growing, contentment is not possible, fulfillment is not possible.

Now you are on the right track. Now things will happen with a faster pace. Speed also is accumulative. If you have watched the spring, first only one flower blooms, and then ten flowers, then hundreds of flowers, and then thousands, and then millions. . . .

Just like that it happens in spiritual growth too. But everybody is stumbling in darkness, groping in darkness. Somebody becomes a poet not knowing whether that is his vocation, his heart's real desire. Somebody becomes a musician not knowing whether that is going to fulfill his life. Somebody becomes a painter. . . . And people have to become something; some earning is needed and one has to do something to prove oneself.

So people go on groping and they become something.

And you are fortunate, Pankaja, that you came to realize that what you were doing was not the real thing for you. There are many unfortunate people—after their whole lives are wasted, then they recognize that they have been into something which was not their real work. They were doing somebody else's work.

I have heard about a famous surgeon, one of the world's most famous surgeons. He was retiring. Even at the age of seventy-five his hands were as young as they had been before. He was able to do brain surgery even at the age of seventy-five; his hands were not yet shaky.

Everybody was happy—his disciples, students, colleagues—and they were celebrating. But he was sad. Somebody asked him, "Why are you sad? You are the world's most famous brain surgeon. You should be happy!"

He said, "Yes, I should be happy, I also think so, but what can I do? I never wanted to be a famous surgeon in the first place. I wanted to be a dancer—and I am the lousiest dancer you can find. My father *forced* me to be a surgeon—and he was right in a way, because by dancing what can you get? The very idea was silly in his eyes, so he forced me to be a surgeon. I became a surgeon, I became famous. Now I am retiring, but I am sad —my whole life has gone down the drain. I never wanted to be a surgeon in the first place, so who cares whether I am famous or not? I would have loved to be just a good dancer, even if unknown, anonymous— that would have been enough."

While questioning a suspect, the police detective leafed through the man's folder. "I see here," he said, "that you have a string of previous arrests. Here is one for armed robbery, breaking and entering, sexual assault, sexual assault, sexual assault. . . ."

"Yes, sir," replied the felon modestly, "it took me a little while to find out what I do best."

Pankaja, you came to me in the right time. Rejoice! Celebrate! And things have started happening. You were like a hard rock when you came; now you are becoming soft like a flower. The spring is not far away.

The fourth question

Bhagwan,
Most religions have a negative attitude
towards work, as if it is a punishment and a
labor and not at all spiritual. Could you
speak to us more about working?

Parmananda,

THE BUDDHAS HAVE ALWAYS BEEN LIFE-AFFIRMATIVE, but the religions that arose afterwards have all been life-negative. This is a strange phenomenon, but there is something which has to be understood—why it happened in the first place. And it happened again and again.

It seems that the moment a Buddha speaks he is bound to be misunderstood. If you don't understand him, that's okay, but people don't stop there: they *mis*-understand him—because people cannot tolerate the idea that they don't understand. It is better to misunderstand than not to understand; at least you have some kind of understanding. All the Buddhas have

been misunderstood, wrongly interpreted. And whatsoever they were standing for has been forgotten as
soon as they were gone, and just the opposite was or-
ganized.

Jesus was a lover of life, a very affirmative person,
but Christianity is life-negative. The seers of the Upanishads were absolutely life-affirmative people, they
loved life tremendously, but Hinduism is life-negative,
Buddhism and Jainism are life-negative.

Just look at the statue of Mahavira and you will see
that he must have loved his body, he must have loved
life and existence. He is so beautiful! It is said about
Mahavira that it is possible that never before and never
again has a more beautiful person walked on the earth.
But look at the Jaina *munis,* the Jaina monks, and you
will find them the ugliest. What has happened?

Buddha is very life-affirmative. Of course, he does
not affirm *your* life, because your life is not life at all; it
is death in disguise. He *condemns* your life, but he af-
firms the real life, the eternal life. But that's how he was
misunderstood. His condemnation of your false life
was taken to be condemnation of life itself. And
nobody bothered that he was affirming life—real life,
eternal life, divine life, the life of the awakened ones.
That is true life. What life do *you* have? It is just a
nightmarish experience. But the Buddhists—the Buddhist monks and nuns—have lived *against* life.

Parmananda, it is because of this misunderstanding,
which seems to be inevitable. . . . I can see it happening with me. Whatsoever I say is immediately misunderstood all over the world. I really enjoy it! Strange,
but somehow seems to be natural. The moment you
say something you can be sure that it is going to be misunderstood, for the simple reason that people are going

to interpret it according to *their* minds. And their minds are fast asleep. They are hearing in their sleep; they can't hear rightly, they can't hear the whole thing. Only fragments they hear.

Even a man like P.D. Ouspensky, who lived with Gurdjieff for years, could not hear the whole teaching as it was. When he wrote his famous book *In Search of the Miraculous* and he showed it to George Gurdjieff, his Master, he said, "It is beautiful, but it needs a subtitle: *Fragments of an Unknown Teaching.*"

Ouspensky said, "But why?—why fragments?"

He said, "Because these are only fragments. What I have told you you have not heard in its totality. And whatsoever you have written is beautiful. . . ."

Ouspensky was really one of the most skillful writers the world has ever known, very artistic, very logical, a superb artist with words.

So he said, "You have written well, you have written beautifully, but these are only fragments—and the fragments cannot reveal the truth. On the contrary, they conceal it. So call it: *Fragments of an Unknown Teaching.* The teaching still remains unknown. You just had a few glimpses here and there, and you have put all those glimpses together, you have somehow made a whole out of them, but it is not the truth, it is not the real teaching."

Ouspensky understood it. Hence the book still carries the subtitle: *Fragments of an Unknown Teaching.*

What to say about ordinary people? Ouspensky cannot be called an ordinary person; extraordinarily intelligent he was. If fact, it was because of him that Gurdjieff became famous in the world; otherwise nobody may have heard about him. His own writings are very difficult to understand. There are very few people in the world who have read *his* books—they are very difficult to read. Gurdjieff writes in such a way that he makes it in every possible way difficult for you to grasp what he is saying, what he wants to say. Sentences go on and on . . . by the time the sentence comes to a full stop you have forgotten the beginning! And he uses words of his own invention which exist nowhere; nobody knows what the meaning of those words is. No dictionary has those words. In fact, they never existed before; he invented them.

And he writes in such a boring way that if you suffer from insomnia they are good, those books. You read three . . . four pages at the most you can read and you are bound to fall asleep. I have never come across a single person who has read his books from the beginning to the end.

When for the first time his first book was published —*All and Everything*—one hundred pages were open and the remaining nine hundred pages were not cut yet. And with a note the book was sold saying, "Read the first hundred pages, the introductory part. If you still feel like reading, then you can open the other pages. Otherwise return the book and take your money back." Even to read those hundred pages is very difficult.

It was a device. It needs great awareness to read. The book is not written to inform you about something; the book is only a device to make you aware. You can read it only if you are very conscious, if you have decided consciously, "I have to go through it from the beginning to the end, and I am not going to fall asleep, and I am not going to stop, whatsoever happens, and whatsoever my mind says I am going to finish it."

If you make that decision . . . and it is very difficult

to keep it for one thousand pages of such nonsense. Yes, here and there there are beautiful truths, but then you will come across those truths only if you go through much nonsense. Gems you will find, but they are few and far between. Once in a while you will come across a diamond, but for that you will have to read fifty, sixty very boring pages.

I have seen thousands of books, but Gurdjieff is extraordinary. Nobody have I seen who can create such boring stuff. But he is deliberately doing it; that was his method.

If you went to see him, the first thing he would tell you was to read fifty pages of his book loudly in front of him. That was the greatest task! You don't understand a single word, a single sentence, and it goes on and on and on, and he sits there looking at you. You have to finish fifty pages, then you can be accepted as a disciple. If you cannot manage this simple feat, then you are rejected.

Ouspensky made him famous in the world, but even Ouspensky could not get to the very core of his teaching—only fragments. And he understood only in part.

And remember always: truth cannot be divided into fragments; you cannot understand only parts of it. Either you understand the whole of it or you don't understand it at all. But it is very difficult to recognize the fact that "I don't understand." And knowledgeable people—scholars, professors—they can*not* accept that *they* don't understand, so they go on misinterpreting.

And the most fatal misinterpretation has been that all affirmative teachings have been turned into negative ones. In fact, you live in a negative darkness. When Buddha speaks he speaks from a positive state of light;

by the time his words reach you they have reached into a negative darkness. Your negative darkness changes the color of those words, the meaning of those words, the connotations of those words, the nuances of those words. And then *you* create the church. You create Christianity, Hinduism, Mohammedanism, Jainism; you create all kinds of "isms" and you create all kinds of religions.

Yes, Parmananda, most religions have a negative attitude towards work because they are against life. Hence they can't be *for* work, they can't be creative. They teach renunciation of life—how can they teach creativity? And they teach that life is a punishment, so how can they say life is spiritual? You are being punished for your past life karmas, that's why you are born. It is a punishment—just as in Soviet Russia if you are punished you are sent to Siberia.

In the days of the British Raj in India, if somebody was to be really punished they used to send him to faraway islands: Andaman, Nicobar. The climate is bad, not healthy at all; no facilities to live, nothing grows, hard work. That was punishment.

All these life-negative religions have been telling you, directly or indirectly, that this earth is like Andaman and Nicobar, or like Siberia, and you are prisoners. You have been thrown here, thrown into life, to be punished. This is utter nonsense.

Life is not a prison, it is a school. You are sent here to learn, you are sent here to grow. You are sent here to become more conscious, more aware. This earth is a great device of God.

This is *my* approach towards life: life is not a punishment but a reward. You are rewarded by being given a

great opportunity to grow, to see, to know, to understand, to be. I call life spiritual. In fact, to me, life and
God are synonymous.

The fifth question

Bhagwan,
Why do Indians think they are more
spiritual than others?

John,

PLEASE FORGIVE THE POOR INDIANS. They don't have
anything else to brag about. You can brag about
other things: money, power, atomic or hydrogen
bombs, airplanes, that you have walked on the moon,
that you have penetrated to the very secrets of life,
your science, technology; you can brag about your affluence. Poor India has nothing else to brag about; it
can only brag about something invisible so there is no
need to prove it. Spirituality is such a thing you can
brag about it and nobody can prove it, nobody can
disprove it.

For thousands of years India has suffered starvation,
poverty, so much so that it has to rationalize it. It has
rationalized it so that to be poor is something spiritual.
The Indian spiritual man renounces all comforts and
becomes poor. When he becomes poor, only then do
Indians recognize him as spiritual. If he does not become poor, how can he be spiritual?

Poverty has become the very foundation of Indian
spirituality. The more poor you are, the more spiritual
you are. Even if you are unhealthy, that is good for be-

ing spiritual; that shows your antagonism towards the body. Torture your body, fast, don't eat, don't fulfill the needs of the body, and you are doing some spiritual work.

So you will look at Indian so-called spiritual saints and many of them will look physically ill, in deep suffering, in self-torture; their faces are pale because of fasting. But if you ask their disciples they will say, "Look, what a golden aura around the face of our saint!" I know such people—just a feverish aura around their faces, nothing else! But their disciples will say, "A golden aura—this is spirituality!"

Count Keyserling writes in his diary that when he came to India he understood for the first time that poverty, starvation, ill health, these are necessary requirements for spirituality. These are rationalizations. And everybody wants to be higher than the other, superior to the other.

Now, there is no other way for Indians to declare their superiority. They cannot compete in science, in technology, in industry, but they can compete in spirituality. They are more able to fast, to starve themselves. For thousands of years they have practiced starvation, so they have become very very accustomed to it; it is easy for them.

For the American to go on a fast is very difficult. Eating five times a day—that means almost the whole day you are eating—and I am not counting things that you eat in between. . . . For the American it is difficult to fast, but for the Indian it has become almost natural. His body has become accustomed to it. The body has a tremendous capacity to adjust itself.

The Indian can sit in the hot sun, almost in a state of fire from the showering of the sun, undisturbed. You cannot sit there—you have become accustomed to air conditioning. The Indian can sit in the cold weather, naked in the Himalayas. *You* cannot; you have become accustomed to central heating. The body becomes accustomed.

And then India can claim: "This is spirituality. Come and compete with us!" And you cannot compete. And certainly, when you cannot compete, you have to bow down to the Indians and you have to accept that they must have some clue. There is no clue, nothing, just a long long history of poverty.

In a cannibal village in the heart of Africa, the wife of the chief head-hunter went to the local butcher's shop in search of a choice rib for her husband's dinner. Inspecting the goods, she asked the butcher, "What is that one?"

The butcher replied, "That is an American—seventy cents a pound."

"Well, then what about that one?" asked the woman.

The butcher replied, "That is an Italian—ninety-five cents a pound. He is a little spicy."

"And," asked the woman, "what about that one there in the corner?"

"He is an Indian," replied the butcher. "two dollars a pound."

The woman gasped, "Two dollars a pound? What makes him so expensive?"

"Well, lady," the butcher replied, "have you ever tried cleaning an Indian?"

But that has become spirituality. Do you know?— Jaina monks never take a bath. To take a bath is thought to be a luxury. They don't clean their teeth; that is thought to be a luxury. Now, to be spiritual in the Jaina sense of the term you have to stop taking a bath, cleaning your teeth, even combing your hair, even cutting your hair. If it becomes too messy, too dirty, you have to pull it out by hand. You can't use any razor or any other mechanical device, because a spiritual person should be independent of all machines. So Jaina monks pull their own hair out. And when a Jaina monk pulls his hair out, mostly once a year, then a great gathering happens because it is thought to be something very special.

I have been to such gatherings. Thousands of Jainas gather together simply to see this poor man, hungry, dirty, pulling his hair out—crazy! And you will see people watching with great joy and with great superiority: "This is our saint! Who *else* can compete with us?"

No nation is spiritual. It has not happened yet. One can hope that it may happen some day, but it has not happened yet. In fact, only individuals can be spiritual, not nations. And individuals have been spiritual all over the world, everywhere. But ignorance prevents people from recognizing others' spirituality.

One day I was talking to an Indian and I told him that everywhere spirituality has been happening; it is nothing to do with India as such.

He said, "But so many saints have happened here. Where else have so many saints happened?"

I said, "Do you know how many saints have happened in China? Just tell me a few names."

He had not even heard of a single name. He does not know anything about Lao Tzu, he does not know about Chuang Tzu, he does not know about Lieh Tzu.

He does not know anything of the long long tradition of Chinese mysticism. But he knows about Nanak, Kabir, Mahavira, Krishna, Buddha, so he thinks all the great saints have happened only in India. That is sheer stupidity. They have happened in Japan, they have happened in Egypt, they have happened in Jerusalem. They have happened everywhere! But you don't know —and you don't want to know either. You simply remain confined to your own sect.

In fact, you may have lived in the neighborhood of the Jainas your whole life, but you cannot tell the twenty-four names of their great *teerthankaras*. Who bothers to know about the others? Only one name— Mahavira—is known; the twenty-three other names are almost unknown. Even Jainas themselves cannot give the twenty-four names in exact sequence. They know three names: the first, Adinatha; the last, Mahavira; and the one before Mahavira, a cousin-brother of Krishna, Neminath. These three are known; the remaining twenty-one are almost unknown even to the Jainas. And this is how it is.

Do you know how many Hassid mystics have attained to God? Do you know how many Zen Masters have attained to Buddhahood? Do you know how many Sufis have attained to the ultimate state? Nobody cares, nobody wants to know. People live in a small, cozy corner of their own religion and they think this is all.

Neither Indians nor anybody else is specially spiritual or holy. Spirituality is something that happens to individuals. It is the individual becoming aflame with God. It has nothing to do with any collectivity—nation, race, church.

The sixth question

Bhagwan,
Why are the Jews so notorious for their
money-greed?

Narotam,

DO YOU THINK OTHERS ARE IN ANY WAY DIFFERENT from the Jews? Unless love flowers in your being you are bound to remain greedy. Greed is the absence of love. If you love, greed disappears; if you don't love, greed remains.

Greed is rooted in fear. And of course, Jews have lived in tremendous fear for centuries. For the two thousand years since Jesus they have lived in constant fear. Fear creates greed. And because they lost their nation—they lost everything, they became uprooted, they became wanderers—the only thing they could trust was money; they could not trust anybody else. Hence, naturally, they became greedy. Don't be too hard on them for that. They are greedy, maybe a little more than others, but that is only a difference of quantity, not of quality.

In India we have *Marwaris,* who are the Indian Jews. Jainas are not less greedy . . . and others too! Maybe they are not so notorious. Jews become notorious because whatsoever they do, they do with a flavor; whatsoever they do, they do without any disguise. They are not very deceptive people—intelligent but not deceptive. Whatsoever they want to do, they do it directly. And they are very earthly people. And that is one of the qualities I appreciate. The earth is our home and we have to be earthly.

A real spirituality must be rooted in earthliness. Any spirituality that denies the earth, rejects the earth, becomes abstract, becomes airy-fairy. It has no more blood in it; it is no more alive. Yes, Jews are very earthbound.

And what is wrong in having money? One should not be possessive; one should be able to use it. And Jews know how to use it! One should not be miserly. Money has to be created and money has to be used. Money is a beautiful invention, a great blessing, if rightly used. It makes many things possible. Money is a magical phenomenon.

If you have a ten-rupee note in your pocket, you have thousands of things in your pocket. You can have anything with those ten rupees. You can materialize a man who will massage your body the whole night! Or you can materialize food or you can materialize *anything!* That ten-rupee note carries many possibilities. You cannot carry all those possibilities with you if there is no note; then your life will be very limited. You can have a man who can massage your body, but then that is the only possibility you have with you. If you suddenly feel hungry or thirsty, then that man cannot do anything else. But a ten-rupee note can do many things, millions of things; it has infinite possibilities. It is one of the greatest inventions of man; there is no need to be against it. *I* am not against it.

Use it. Don't cling to it. Clinging is bad. The more you cling to money, the poorer the world becomes because of your clinging, because money is multiplied if it is always moving from one hand to another hand.

In English we have another name for money which is more significant—it is "currency." That simply indicates that money should always remain moving like a current. It should always be on the move from one hand to another hand. The more it moves the better.

For example, if I have a ten-rupee note and I keep it to myself, then there is only one ten-rupee note in the world. If I give it to you and you give it to somebody else and each person goes on giving, if it goes through ten hands then we have a hundred rupees, we have used a hundred rupees' worth of utilities; the ten rupees is multiplied by ten.

And Jews know how to use money; nothing is wrong in it. Yes, greed is bad. Greed means you become obsessed with money; you don't use it as a means, it becomes the end. That is bad, and it is bad whether you are a Jew or a Jaina, Hindu or Mohammedan; it doesn't matter.

Four Jewish mothers were talking, naturally of their sons.

One said, "My son is studying to be a doctor, and when he graduates he will make $50,000 a year."

Said the second, "My son is studying dentistry, and when he graduates he will make $100,000 a year."

The third said, "My son is studying to be a psychoanalyst, and when he graduates he will make $200,000 a year."

The fourth one remained silent. The other ones asked her, "And what about your son?"

"He is studying to become a rabbi," she answered.

"And how much does a rabbi make?"

"$10,000 a year."

"$10,000? Is this a job for a Jewish boy?"

Gropestein's clothing store stood on New York's Lower East Side. One day, Gropestein went out for lunch and left Salter, his new salesman, in charge.

When he came back Salter proudly announced, "I sold that black cloth coat."

"For how much?" asked Gropestein.

"Ninety-eight cents, like it said on the tag."

"Ninety-eight cents?" screamed the owner. "The tag said ninety-eight dollars, you idiot!"

The clerk looked as if he would die of embarrassment.

"Let this be a lesson to you," said Gropestein. "But don't feel bad—we made ten percent profit."

A famous anti-Semite was dying. He gathered his sons around his deathbed and said, "Sons, my last wish and command is that whenever you need anything, go buy it from a Jew and give him the first price he asks."

The sons in surprise said, "Father, has your mind gone crazy in this your last hour?"

"Ah, no," smiled the anti-Semite wickedly, "he is going to eat himself up he has not asked for more."

The seventh question

Bhagwan,
What is the future of morality concerning sex?

Divendra,

T HERE IS NO FUTURE OF ANY MORALITY concerning sex. In fact, the very combination of sex and morality has poisoned the whole past of morality. Morality became so much sex-oriented that it lost all other dimensions—which are far more important. Sex should not really be so much of a concern for moral thinking.

Truth, sincerity, authenticity, totality—these things

should be the real concerns of morality. Consciousness, meditation, awareness, love, compassion—these should be the real concerns of morality.

But sex and morality became almost synonymous in the past; sex became overpowering, overwhelming. So whenever you say somebody is immoral you simply mean that something is wrong with his sexual life. And when you say somebody is a very moral person, all that you mean is that he follows the rules of sexuality laid down by the society in which he lives. Morality became one-dimensional; it has not been good. There is no future for that morality; that is dying. In fact, it is dead. You are carrying a corpse.

Sex should be more fun than such a serious affair as it has been made in the past. It should be like a game, a play: two persons playing with each other's bodily energies. If they both are happy, it should be nobody else's concern. They are not harming anybody; they are simply rejoicing in each other's energy. It is a dance of two energies together. It should not be a concern of the society at all. Unless somebody interferes in somebody else's life—imposes himself, forces somebody, is violent, violates somebody's life, then only should society come in. Otherwise there is no problem; it should not be any concern at all.

The future will have a totally different vision of sex. It will be more fun, more joy, more friendship, more a play than a serious affair as it has been in the past. It has destroyed people's lives, has burdened them so much —unnecessarily! It has created so much jealousy, possessiveness, domination, nagging, quarrelling, fighting, condemnation—for *no* reason at all.

Sexuality is a simple, biological phenomenon. It should not be given so much importance. Its only significance is that the energy can be transformed into higher planes; it can become more and more spiritual. And the way to make it more spiritual is to make it a less serious affair.

Doctor Biber was perplexed by the case at hand. He had given the sorority girl all sorts of tests, but his results were still inconclusive. "I am not sure what it is," he finally admitted. "You either have a cold or you are pregnant."

"I must be pregnant," said the girl. "I don't know anybody who could have given me a cold."

This is something of the future.

Clarice and Sheffield were having a mid-afternoon breakfast. Their Park Avenue apartment was completely askew after a wild, all-night party.

"Dear, this is rather embarrassing," said Sheffield, "but was it you I made love to in the library last night?"

"About what time?" asked Clarice.

Another story about the future:

The schoolteacher was complaining rather bitterly to Cornelia about the behavior of little Nathaniel. "He is always picking on boys smaller than he is and beating them up," she said.

"My goodness!" said Cornelia, "That boy is just like his pappy."

"And several times I have caught him in the cloak-room with one of the little girls," continued the teacher.

"Just the sort of thing his pappy would do."

"Not only that, but he steals things from the other children."

"The very same as his pappy—Lord, I sure am glad I didn't marry that man!"

Don't be worried about the future of morality concerning sex. It is going to disappear completely. The future will know a totally different vision of sex. And once sex no longer overwhelms morality so powerfully, morality will be free to have some other concerns which are far more important.

Truth, sincerity, honesty, totality, compassion, service, meditation, these should be the real concerns of morality—because these are things which transform your life, these are things which bring you closer to God.

And the last question

Bhagwan,
Why do you speak at all if the truth is
inexpressible?

Paramahansa,

TAKE NO NOTICE!

Books on Bhagwan

BHAGWAN: NOTITIES VAN EEN DISCIPEL
by Swami Deva Amrito (Jan Foudraine) –(Ankh-Hermes)
BHAGWAN SHREE RAJNEESH: DE LAATSTE GOK
by Ma Satya Bharti –(Mirananda)
OORSPRONGELIJK GEZICHT, EIN GANG NAAR HUIS
by Swami Deva Amrito (Jan Foudraine) –(Ambo)

FRENCH

L'EVEIL A LA CONSCIENCE COSMIQUE —*(Dangles)*
JE SUIS LA PORTE —*(EPI)*
LE LIVRE DES SECRETS (volume I) —*(Soleil Orange)*
LA MEDITATION DYNAMIQUE —*(Dangles)*

GERMAN

Translations

AUF DER SUCHE —*(Sambuddha Verlag)*
DAS BUCH DER GEHEIMNISSE (volume I) —*(Heyne Verlag)*
DAS ORANGENE BUCH —*(Sambuddha Verlag)*
EKSTASE: DIE VERGESSENE SPRACHE —*(Herzschlag Verlag, formerly Ki-Buch)*
ESOTERISCHE PSYCHOLOGIE —*(Rajneesh Verlag)*
ICH BIN DER WEG —*(Rajneesh Verlag)*
INTELLIGENZ DES HERZENS —*(Herzschlag Verlag, formerly Ki-Buch)*
KEIN WASSER KEIN MOND —*(Herzschlag Verlag, formerly Ki-Buch)*
KOMM UND FOLGE MIR —*(Sannyas Verlag)*
MEDITATION: DIE KUNST ZU SICH SELBST ZU FINDEN —*(Heyne Verlag)*
MEIN WEG: DER WEG DER WEISSEN WOLKE —*(Herzschlag Verlag, formerly
Ki-Buch)*
MIT WURZELN UND MIT FLÜGELN —*(Lotos Verlag)*
DAS HIMMELREICH GLEICHT EINEM SENFKORN —*(Fischer)*
NICHT BEVOR DU STIRBST —*(Edition Gyandip, Switzerland)*
DIE SCHUHE AUF DEM KOPF —*(Lotos Verlag)*
SPIRITUELLE ENTWICKLUNG —*(Fischer)*
SPRENGT DEN FELS DER UNBEWUSSTHEIT —*(Fischer)*
TANTRA: DIE HÖCHSTE EINSICHT —*(Sambuddha Verlag)*
TANTRISCHE LIEBESKUNST —*(Sannyas Verlag)*
DIE VERBORGENE HARMONIE —*(Sannyas Verlag)*
WAS IST MEDITATION? —*(Sannyas Verlag)*

Books on Bhagwan

BEGEGNUNG MIT NIEMAND
by Mascha Rabben (Ma Hari Chetana) –(Herzschlag Verlag)
GANZ ENTSPANNT IM HIER UND JETZT
by Swami Satyananda –(Rowohlt)

IM GRUNDE IST ALLES GANZ EINFACH
by Swami Satyananda—(Ullstein)
WAGNIS ORANGE
by Ma Satya Bharti—(Fachbuchhandlung fur Psychologie)

GREEK
I KRIFI ARMONIA——(Emmanual Rassoulis) THE HIDDEN HARMONY

HEBREW
TANTRA: THE SUPREME UNDERSTANDING——*(Massada)*

ITALIAN

Translations
L'ARMONIA NASCOSTA (volumes 1 & 2)——*(Re Nudo)*
DIECI STORIE ZEN DI BHAGWAN SHREE RAJNEESH (NÉ ACQUA, NÉ LUNA)
——*(Il Fiore d'Oro)*
IO SONO LA SOGLIA——*(Mediterranee)*
IL LIBRO DEI SEGRETI——*(Bompiani)*
MEDITAZIONE DINAMICA: L'ARTE DELL'ESTASI INTERIORE——*(Mediterranee)*
LA RIVOLUZIONE INTERIORE——*(Armenia)*
LA RICERCA——*(La Salamandra)*
IL SEME DELLA RIBELLIONE (volumes 1, 2 & 3)——*(Re Nudo)*
TANTRA: LA COMPRENSIONE SUPREMA——*(Bompiani)*
TAO: I TRE TESORI (volumes 1, 2 & 3)——*(Re Nudo)*
TECNICHE DI LIBERAZIONE——*(La Salamandra)*
SEMI DI SAGGEZZA——*(SugarCo)*

Books on Bhagwan
ALLA RICERCA DEL DIO PERDUTO
by Swami Deva Majid—(SurgarCo)
IL GRANDE ESPERIMENTO: MEDITAZIONI E TERAPIE NELL'ASHRAM DI
BHAGWAN SHREE RAJNEESH
by Ma Satya Bharti—(Armenia)
L'INCANTO D'ARANCIO
by Swami Swatantra Sarjano—(Savelli)

JAPANESE
THE MUSTARD SEED——*(Merkmal)*
UNTIL YOU DIE——*(Fumikura)*
THE EMPTY BOAT——*(Rajneesh Publications)*
THE HEART SUTRA——*(Merkmal)*
THE GRASS GROWS BY ITSELF——*(Fumikura)*
THE SEARCH——*(Merkmal)*
MY WAY: THE WAY OF THE WHITE CLOUDS——*(Rajneesh Publications)*
THE SECRET——*(Merkmal)*

DANCE YOUR WAY TO GOD—(Rajneesh Publications)
FROM SEX TO SUPERCONSCIOUSNESS—(Rajneesh Publications)
MEDITATION: THE ART OF ECSTASY—(Merkmal)
TANTRA THE SUPREME UNDERSTANDING—(Merkmal)
TAO: THE THREE TREASURES (volumes 1-4)—(Merkmal)

PORTUGUESE (BRAZIL)
O CIPRESTE NO JARDIM—(Soma)
EU SOU A PORTA—(Pensamento)
MEDITACÃO: A ARTE DO ÊXTASE—(Cultrix)
MEU CAMINHO: O COMAINHO DAS NUVENS BRANCAS—
(Tao Livraria & Editora)
NEM AGUA, NEM LUA—(Pensamento)
O LIVRO ORANGE—(Soma)
PALAVRAS DE FOGO—(Global/Ground)
A PSICOLOGIA DO ESOTÉRICO—(Tao Livraria & Editora)
A SEMENTE DE MOSTARDA (volumes 1 & 2)— (Tao Livraria & Editora)
TANTRA: SEXO E ESPIRITUALIDADE—(Agora)
TANTRA: A SUPREMA COMPREENSÃO—(Cultrix)
ANTES QUE VOCE MORRA—(Maha Lakshmi Editora)

SPANISH

Translations
INTRODUCCIÓN AL MUNDO DEL TANTRA—(Colección Tantra)
MEDITACIÓN: EL ARTE DEL EXTASIS—(Colección Tantra)
PSICOLOGIA DE LO ESOTÉRICO: LA NUEVA EVOLUCIÓN DEL HOMBRE—
(Cuatro Vientos Editorial)
¿QUE ES MEDITACIÓN?—(Koan/Rosellò Impresions)
YO SOY LA PUERTA—(Editorial Diana)
SOLO UN CIELO, 1 and 2—(Colección Tantra)

Books on Bhagwan
IL RIESGO SUPREMO
by Ma Satya Bharti –(Martinez Roca)

SWEDISH
DEN VÄLDIGA UTMANINGEN—(Livskraft)

RAJNEESH MEDITATION CENTERS, ASHRAMS AND COMMUNES

There are hundreds of Rajneesh meditation centers throughout the world. These are some of the main ones, which can be contacted for the name and address of the center nearest you. They can also tell you about the availability of the books of Bhagwan Shree Rajneesh — in English or in foreign language editions. General information is available from Rajneesh Foundation International.

USA

RAJNEESH FOUNDATION INTERNATIONAL
Rajneeshpuram, OR 97741. Tel: (503) 489-3301
DEEPTA RAJNEESH MEDITATION CENTER
3024 Ashby Avenue, Berkeley, CA 94705. Tel: (415) 845-2515
GEETAM RAJNEESH SANNYAS ASHRAM
Box 576, Lucerne Valley, CA 92356. Tel: (714) 248-7301
SAMBODHI RAJNEESH SANNYAS ASHRAM
Conomo Point Road, Essex, MA 01929. Tel: (617) 768-7640

CANADA

ARVIND RAJNEESH SANNYAS ASHRAM
2807 W. 16th Ave., Vancouver, B.C. V5Z 1R9. Tel: 604-734-4681
SATDHARM RAJNEESH MEDITATION CENTER
184 Madison Avenue, Toronto, Ontario M5R 2S5. Tel: (416) 968-2194
SHANTI SADAN RAJNEESH MEDITATION CENTER
1817 Rosemont, Montreal,
Quebec H2G 1S5. Tel: (514) 272-4566

AUSTRIA

PRADEEP RAJNEESH MEDITATION CENTER
Siebenbrunnenfeldgasse 4, 1050 Vienna. Tel: 524-860

AUSTRALIA

PREMDWEEP RAJNEESH MEDITATION CENTER
64 Fullerton Rd., Norwood, S.A. 5067. Tel: 08-423388
SAHAJAM RAJNEESH SANNYAS ASHRAM
8 Collie Street, Fremantle 6160, W.A. Tel: (09) 336-2422
SATPRAKASH RAJNEESH MEDITATION CENTER
108 Oxford Street, Darlinghurst 2010, N.S.W. Tel: (02) 336570
SVARUP RAJNEESH MEDITATION CENTER
9 Canning St., 169 Elgin St., Carlton. Victoria. Tel: 347-6274

BELGIUM

VADAN RAJNEESH MEDITATION CENTER
Platte-Lo-Straat, 3200 Leuven (Kessel-Lo). Tel: 016/25-1487

BRAZIL
SOMA RAJNEESH MEDITATION CENTER
Rua Roque Petrella 542, Brooklyn CEP 04581, Sao Paulo SP. Tel: 240-2928

CHILE
SAGARO RAJNEESH MEDITATION CENTER
Paula Jaraquemada 297, La Reina, Santiago. Tel: 227-1751

DENMARK
ANAND NIKETAN RAJNEESH MEDITATION CENTER
Strøget, Frederiksberggade 15, 1459 Copenhagen K. Tel: (01) 117909

EAST AFRICA
ANAND NEED RAJNEESH MEDITATION CENTER
Kitisuru Estate, P.O. Box 72424, Nairobi, Kenya. Tel: 582600

FRANCE
PRADIP RAJNEESH MEDITATION CENTER
13 Rue Bichat, 75010 Paris. Tel: 607-9559

GREAT BRITAIN
KALPTARU RAJNEESH MEDITATION CENTER
28 Oak Village, London NW5 4QN. Tel: (01) 267-8304
MEDINA RAJNEESH NEO-SANNYAS COMMUNE
Herringswell, Bury St. Edmunds, Suffolk IP28 6SW. Tel: (0638) 750234
GOURISHANKAR RAJNEESH MEDITATION CENTER
43 Iverleitch Row, Edinburgh, Scotland. Tel: 031-552-3993

HOLLAND
DE STAD RAJNEESH NEO-SANNYAS COMMUNE
Kamperweg 80-86 8191 KC Heerde. Tel: 05207-1261
GRADA RAJNEESH NEO-SANNYAS COMMUNE
Prins Hendrikstraat 64, 1931 BK Egmond aan Zee. Tel: 02206-4114

INDIA
RAJNEESHDHAM
17 Koregaon Park, Poona 411 001. Tel: 28127
RAJ YOGA RAJNEESH MEDITATION CENTER
C 5/44 Safdarjang Development Area, New Delhi 100 016. Tel: 654533

ITALY
CITTA DI RAJNEESH NEO-SANNYAS COMMUNE
15036 Villabella di Valenza Po, (AL). Tel: (0131) 953993
MIASTO RAJNEESH NEO-SANNYAS COMMUNE
Podere S. Giorgio, Cotorniano 53010, Frosini (Siena) Tel: 0577-960124
VIVEK RAJNEESH MEDITATION CENTER
Via Castelfidardo 7, 20121 Milan. Tel: 659-5632

JAPAN
SHANTIYUGA RAJNEESH MEDITATION CENTER
Sky Mansion 2F, 1-34-1 Ookayama, Meguro-ku, Tokyo 152. Tel: (03) 724-9631
UTSAVA RAJNEESH MEDITATION CENTER
7-19-34 Morikita Cho, Higashinada-KU, Kobe 658. Tel: 078-411-8319

NEW ZEALAND
SHANTI NIKETAN RAJNEESH MEDITATION CENTER
115 Symonds Street. Auckland. Tel: 770-326

PHILIPPINES
PREM SADAN RAJNEESH MEDITATION CENTER
39 Captain Guido Street, Heroes Hill, Quezon City 3010. Tel: 965 410

SWEDEN
DEEVA RAJNEESH MEDITATION CENTER
Surbrunnsgatan 60, 11327 Stockholm. Tel: (08) 327788

SWITZERLAND
GYANDIP RAJNEESH MEDITATION CENTER
Baumackerstr. 42, 8050 Zurich. Tel: (01) 312 1600

WEST GERMANY
ANAND SAGAR RAJNEESH SANNYAS ASHRAM
Lutticherstr. 33/35, 5 Koln 1. Tel: 0221-517199
DHARMADEEP RAJNEESH SANNYAS ASHRAM
Karolinenstr. 7-9, c/o Lorien, 2000 Hamburg 6. Tel: (040) 432140
RAJNEESHSTADT NEO-SANNYAS COMMUNE
Schloss Wolfsbrunnen, 3466 Meinhard. Tel: (05651) 70217
SATDHARMA RAJNEESH MEDITATION CENTER
Klensestr. 41, 8000 Munich 2. Tel: 089-282-113
VIHAN RAJNEESH SANNYAS COMMUNE
Urbanstr. 64, 1000 Berlin 61. Tel: (030) 691-2051

BOOKS PUBLISHED BY
RAJNEESH FOUNDATION INTERNATIONAL

THE DISCOURSES OF BHAGWAN SHREE RAJNEESH

Early Discourses
A CUP OF TEA
letters to disciples
FROM SEX TO SUPERCONSCIOUSNESS

The Bauls
THE BELOVED (2 volumes)

Buddha
THE BOOK OF THE BOOKS (volume 1)
the Dhammapada
THE DIAMOND SUTRA
the Vajrachchedika Prajnaparamita Sutra
THE DISCIPLINE OF TRANSCENDENCE (4 volumes)
the Sutra of 42 Chapters
THE HEART SUTRA
the Prajnaparamita Hridayam Sutra

Buddhist Masters
THE WHITE LOTUS
the sayings of Bodhidharma

Hasidism
THE ART OF DYING
THE TRUE SAGE

Jesus
COME FOLLOW ME (4 volumes)
the sayings of Jesus
I SAY UNTO YOU (2 volumes)
the sayings of Jesus

Kabir
THE DIVINE MELODY
ECSTASY: THE FORGOTTEN LANGUAGE
THE FISH IN THE SEA IS NOT THIRSTY
THE GUEST
THE PATH OF LOVE
THE REVOLUTION

Response to Questions
BE STILL AND KNOW
THE GOOSE IS OUT

MY WAY: THE WAY OF THE WHITE CLOUDS
WALKING IN ZEN, SITTING IN ZEN
WALK WITHOUT FEET, FLY WITHOUT WINGS
     AND THINK WITHOUT MIND
ZEN: ZEST, ZIP, ZAP AND ZING

Sufism
JUST LIKE THAT
THE PERFECT MASTER (2 volumes)
THE SECRET
SUFIS: THE PEOPLE OF THE PATH (2 volumes)
UNIO MYSTICA (2 volumes)
the Hadiqa of Hakim Sanai
UNTIL YOU DIE
THE WISDOM OF THE SANDS (2 volumes)

Tantra
THE BOOK OF THE SECRETS (volumes 4 and 5)
Vigyana Bhairava Tantra
THE TANTRA VISION (2 volumes)
the Royal Song of Saraha
THE BOOKS OF WISDOM (volume 1)
Atisha's Seven Points of Mind Training

Tao
THE EMPTY BOAT
the stories of Chuang Tzu
THE SECRET OF SECRETS (volume 1)
the Secret of the Golden Flower
TAO: THE PATHLESS PATH (2 volumes)
the stories of Lieh Tzu
TAO: THE THREE TREASURES (4 volumes)
the Tao Te Ching of Lao Tzu
WHEN THE SHOE FITS
the stories of Chuang Tzu

The Upanishads
THE ULTIMATE ALCHEMY (2 volumes)
Atma Pooja Upanishad
VEDANTA: SEVEN STEPS TO SAMADHI
Akshya Upanishad

Western Mystics
THE HIDDEN HARMONY
the fragments of Heraclitus
THE NEW ALCHEMY: TO TURN YOU ON
Mabel Collins' Light on the Path
PHILOSOPHIA PERENNIS (2 volumes)
the Golden Verses of Pythagoras

Yoga

YOGA: THE ALPHA AND THE OMEGA (10 volumes)
the Yoga Sutras of Patanjali

Zen

AH, THIS!
ANCIENT MUSIC IN THE PINES
AND THE FLOWERS SHOWERED
DANG DANG DOKO DANG
THE FIRST PRINCIPLE
THE GRASS GROWS BY ITSELF
NIRVANA: THE LAST NIGHTMARE
NO WATER NO MOON
RETURNING TO THE SOURCE
A SUDDEN CLASH OF THUNDER
THE SUN RISES IN THE EVENING
ZEN: THE PATH OF PARADOX (3 volumes)

Zen Masters

NEITHER THIS NOR THAT
Sosan's Hsin Hsin Ming
THE SEARCH
the Ten Bulls of Zen
TAKE IT EASY (2 volumes)
poems of Ikkyu
THIS VERY BODY THE BUDDHA
Hakuin's Song of Meditation

INTIMATE DIALOGUES between the Master and His disciples

HAMMER ON THE ROCK —*(December 10, 1975-January 15, 1976)*
ABOVE ALL DON'T WOBBLE —*(January 16-February 12, 1976)*
NOTHING TO LOSE BUT YOUR HEAD —*(February 13-March 12, 1976)*
BE REALISTIC: PLAN FOR A MIRACLE —*(March 13-April 6, 1976)*
GET OUT OF YOUR OWN WAY —*(April 7-May 2, 1976)*
BELOVED OF MY HEART —*(May 3-May 28, 1976)*
THE CYPRESS IN THE COURTYARD —*(May 29-June 27, 1976)*
A ROSE IS A ROSE IS A ROSE —*(June 28-July 27, 1976)*
DANCE YOUR WAY TO GOD —*(July 28-August 20, 1976)*
THE PASSION FOR THE IMPOSSIBLE —*(August 21-September 18, 1976)*
THE GREAT NOTHING —*(September 19-October 11, 1976)*
GOD IS NOT FOR SALE —*(October 12-November 7, 1976)*
THE SHADOW OF THE WHIP —*(November 8-December 3, 1976)*
BLESSED ARE THE IGNORANT —*(December 4-December 31, 1976)*

THE BUDDHA DISEASE —(January 1977)
WHAT IS, IS, WHAT AIN'T, AIN'T —(February 1977)
THE ZERO EXPERIENCE —(March 1977)
FOR MADMEN ONLY
       (PRICE OF ADMISSION: YOUR MIND)—(April 1977)
THIS IS IT —(May 1977)
THE FURTHER SHORE —(June 1977)
FAR BEYOND THE STARS —(July 1977)
THE NO BOOK
       (NO BUDDHA, NO TEACHING, NO DISCIPLINE)—(August 1977)
DON'T JUST DO SOMETHING, SIT THERE —(September 1977)
ONLY LOSERS CAN WIN IN THIS GAME —(October 1977)
THE OPEN SECRET —(November 1977)
THE OPEN DOOR—(December 1977)
THE SUN BEHIND THE SUN BEHIND THE SUN—(January 1978)
BELIEVING THE IMPOSSIBLE BEFORE BREAKFAST —(February 1978)
DON'T BITE MY FINGER, LOOK WHERE I AM POINTING—(March 1978)
LET GO!—(April 1978)
THE NINETY-NINE NAMES OF NOTHINGNESS—(May 1978)
THE MADMAN'S GUIDE TO ENLIGHTENMENT —(June 1978)
HALLELUJAH!—(August 1978)
THE TONGUE-TIP TASTE OF TAO —(October 1978)
TURN ON, TUNE IN, AND DROP THE LOT —(December 1978)
ZORBA THE BUDDHA —(January 1979)
THE SOUND OF ONE HAND CLAPPING —(March 1981)

OTHER TITLES

THE ORANGE BOOK
       (THE MEDITATION TECHNIQUES OF BHAGWAN SHREE RAJNEESH)
THE RAJNEESH NOTHING BOOK
200 blank pages to play with
THE SOUND OF RUNNING WATER
a photobiography of Bhagwan Shree Rajneesh and His work

BOOKS FROM OTHER PUBLISHERS

EDITIONS IN ENGLISH

UNITED KINGDOM

THE ART OF DYING —*(Sheldon Press)*
THE BOOK OF THE SECRETS (volume 1)—*(Thames & Hudson)*
DIMENSIONS BEYOND THE KNOWN —*(Sheldon Press)*
THE HIDDEN HARMONY —*(Sheldon Press)*
MEDITATION: THE ART OF ECSTASY —*(Sheldon Press)*
THE MUSTARD SEED —*(Sheldon Press)*
NEITHER THIS NOR THAT —*(Sheldon Press)*
NO WATER NO MOON —*(Sheldon Press)*
ROOTS AND WINGS —*(Routledge & Kegan Paul)*
STRAIGHT TO FREEDOM (Original title: UNTIL YOU DIE)—*(Sheldon Press)*
THE SUPREME DOCTRINE —*(Routledge & Kegan Paul)*
THE SUPREME UNDERSTANDING (Original title: TANTRA: THE SUPREME
UNDERSTANDING)—*(Sheldon Press)*
TAO: THE THREE TREASURES (volume 1)—*(Wildwood House)*

Books on Bhagwan

DEATH COMES DANCING: CELEBRATING LIFE
WITH BHAGWAN SHREE RAJNEESH
by Ma Satya Bharti–(Routledge & Kegan Paul)
THE ULTIMATE RISK
by Ma Satya Bharti–(Wildwood House)

UNITED STATES OF AMERICA

THE BOOK OF THE SECRETS (volumes 1, 2 & 3)—*(Harper & Row)*
THE GREAT CHALLENGE —*(Grove Press)*
HAMMER ON THE ROCK—*(Grove Press)*
I AM THE GATE —*(Harper & Row)*
JOURNEY TOWARD THE HEART (Original title: UNTIL YOU DIE)
—*(Harper & Row)*
MEDITATION: THE ART OF ECSTASY —*(Harper & Row)*
THE MUSTARD SEED —*(Harper & Row)*
MY WAY: THE WAY OF THE WHITE CLOUDS —*(Grove Press)*
ONLY ONE SKY (Original title: TANTRA: THE SUPREME UNDERSTANDING)
—*(Dutton)*
THE PSYCHOLOGY OF THE ESOTERIC —*(Harper & Row)*
ROOTS AND WINGS —*(Routledge & Kegan Paul)*
THE SUPREME DOCTRINE —*(Routledge & Kegan Paul)*
WORDS LIKE FIRE (Original title: COME FOLLOW ME, volume 1)
—*(Harper & Row)*

Books on Bhagwan

THE AWAKENED ONE: THE LIFE AND WORK OF
    BHAGWAN SHREE RAJNEESH
by Vasant Joshi—(Harper & Row)

DEATH COMES DANCING: CELEBRATING LIFE WITH BHAGWAN
SHREE RAJNEESH
by Ma Satya Bharti—(Routledge & Kegan Paul)

DRUNK ON THE DIVINE
by Ma Satya Bharti—(Grove Press)

DYING FOR ENLIGHTENMENT
by Bernard Gunther (Swami Deva Amitprem)—(Harper & Row)

NEO-TANTRA
by Bernard Gunther (Swami Deva Amitprem)—(Harper & Row)

FOREIGN LANGUAGE EDITIONS

DANISH

Translations

HEMMELIGHEDERNES BOG (volume 1)—*(Borgens Forlag)*
HU-MEDITATION OG KOSMISK ORGASME—*(Borgens Forlag)*

Books on Bhagwan

SJAELENS OPRØR
by Swami Deva Satyarthi—(Borgens Forlag)

DUTCH

Translations

HET BOEK DER GEHEIMEN (volumes 1, 2 & 3)—*(Mirananda)*
GEEN WATER, GEEN MAAN—*(Mirananda)*
GEZAAID IN GOEDE AARDE—*(Ankh-Hermes)*
IK BEN DE POORT—*(Ankh-Hermes)*
MEDITATIE: DE KUNST VAN INNERLIJKE EXTASE—*(Mirananda)*
MIJN WEG, DE WEG VAN DE WITTE WOLK—*(Arcanum)*
HET MOSTERDZAAD (volumes 1 & 2)—*(Mirananda)*
HET ORANJE MEDITATIEBOEK—*(Ankh-Hermes)*
PSYCHOLOGIE EN EVOLUTIE—*(Ankh-Hermes)*
TANTRA: HET ALLERHOOGSTE INZICHT—*(Ankh-Hermes)*
TANTRA, SPIRITUALITEIT EN SEKS—*(Ankh-Hermes)*
DE TANTRA VISIE (volume 1)—*(Arcanum)*
TAU—*(Ankh-Hermes)*
TOTDAT JE STERFT—*(Ankh-Hermes)*
DE VERBORGEN HARMONIE—*(Mirananda)*
VOLG MIJ—*(Ankh-Hermes)*
ZOEKEN NAAR DE STIER—*(Ankh-Hermes)*
DRINK MIJ—*(Ankh-Hermes)*